Manual for Be
A Compre
Interpreting i.

Practice exercises for beginning interpreters with examples from real court settings in English and Spanish, including colloquialisms from Sonora, Mexico and an asylum hearing sample

Oliver Strömmuse

Anthony Tell Ltd Co
Albuquerque, NM

Praise for *Manual for Beginning Interpreters: A Comprehensive Guide to Interpreting in Immigration Courts*

Strömmuse's approachable and direct manual assists new interpreters in preparing for real hearings in U.S. immigration courts. He makes clear that he wrote this manual—which offers realistic but fictional bilingual transcripts presenting defendants from Sonora, Mexico—because help is urgently needed: "The beginning interpreter lacks training and study materials to start doing the complex job of interpreting in immigration courts," he notes. Opening with the story of a Spanish teacher whose friend invited her to interpret in immigration court, the manual both invites and forewarns readers into the reality of this high-demand but stressful job. Later sections demystify court proceedings, explaining "master calendar hearings," a common, varied, and challenging situation which might sometimes involve interpreting for up to fifty people, or illuminating the processes of individual hearings.

Strömmuse makes a persuasive case for the urgency of this role, noting that in most U.S. immigration courts, "Without the presence of a bilingual lawyer or family member, no one else can correct a mistake." He supplements clear-eyed accounts of an interpreter's role with practical tips ("Always interpret in the first person. For example: 'I am Margarita' or 'I am Ángel.') plus sample vignettes that offer opportunities to practice interpreting and demonstrate "the rigor, seriousness and high standard" expected of court interpreters. Abbreviated but not brief, one sample script covering direct and cross examinations comprises over half the manual's pages. As in a real proceeding, questions are posed in English, while the answers come in Spanish.

An accurate representation of how attorneys organize their examinations, that hearing is organized into "blocks." In other ways, too, the manual simulates actual court practice, demanding that readers practice simultaneous, consecutive and sight interpreting of legal terminology. The committed bilingual reader will follow along, aided by a glossary of terms and links to court documents for study. This manual will serve the beginning interpreter almost as well as real experience.

An inviting and practical introduction to the vital role of interpreter in immigration court.

—BookLife Reviews

Disclaimer: This manual is not intended, nor should it be construed in any way, as legal advice. The characters and narratives used in this book are all fictional, created for teaching purposes only. The PSGs mentioned during "The Hearing" do not represent a legally accurate basis for the asylum claimed presented. They are fictional illustrations of the PSG concept presented for the sole purpose of language and interpretation practice. Note that they might not reflect the reality of an actual asylum case.

Publisher's Cataloging-In-Publication Data
(Prepared by The Donohue Group, Inc.)

Names: Strömmuse, Oliver, author.
Title: Manual for beginning interpreters : a comprehensive guide
    to interpreting in immigration courts : practice exercises for
    beginning interpreters with examples from real court settings
    in English and Spanish, including colloquialisms from
    Sonora, Mexico and an asylum hearing sample / Oliver
    Strömmuse.
Description: [First edition]. | Albuquerque, NM : Anthony Tell
    Ltd Co, 2021. | Includes bibliographical references.
Identifiers: ISBN 9781736215609 (paperback) | ISBN
    9781736215616 (ebook)
Subjects: LCSH: Translating and interpreting--United States--
    Handbooks, manuals, etc. | Translating and interpreting--
    United States--Problems, exercises, etc. | English language--
    Translating--Problems, exercises, etc. | Spanish language--
    Translating--Problems, exercises, etc. | Immigration courts--
    United States. | LCGFT: Handbooks and manuals.
Classification: LCC P306.8.U6 S77 2021 (print) | LCC P306.8.U6
    (ebook) | DDC 418.020973--dc23

To request permissions, contact the publisher at
manualvolume1@protonmail.com.

Paperback: ISBN 978-1-7362156-0-9
Ebook: ISBN 978-1-7362156-1-6

First paperback edition 2021

Quantity discounts are available for immigration law clinics, legal aid societies, legal advocacy organizations, law schools, schools of translation and interpretation, schools of continuing education, adult education, interpreting agencies, dual-language programs, researchers, academics and other institutions for resale, teaching, or gifts. Please contact: manualvolume1@protonmail.com.

Published by Anthony Tell Ltd Co.

Table of Contents

Introduction

Starting out

Reina started out as a Spanish teacher. One night, years ago, Reina had the good fortune to see her artist husband, Timothy, in action while he interpreted for a crowd of Americans and Hispanics at an art happening he had curated. He was conducting a live survey and he wanted to make sure everyone followed along. Reina couldn't believe her eyes. She knew he'd been feeling under the weather but in spite of that, he was fluid, quick and precise in his interpretations, ably bridging the gaps between English and Spanish. Her husband was a natural interpreter!

Soon thereafter, Reina started teaching Spanish for medical personnel at a medical center, where she found herself being asked to interpret for doctors, nurses and staff. She fell in love with interpreting and decided to get certified so she could get an official job as an interpreter.

Even though her teaching engagements continued growing, becoming an interpreter remained her goal. When she learned of the medical interpreting program at a local college, she jumped at the opportunity. It was wonderful. The teachers were great, committed and very encouraging. They often brought in presenters to show a vast array of interpreting techniques, such as *simultaneous interpreting*. When she saw an interpreter demonstrate her simultaneous skills, Reina was sold. She said to herself, "I've got to learn that technique." Up to that point her highest goal had been to emulate the two hours of impromptu *consecutive interpreting* she'd seen her husband do years ago. But now she had a new challenge: not only to learn all the medical terminology but also to be able to retrieve that information so fast that she could simultaneously convert the message from doctors and nurses in real time. After two years of rigorous training, she was on her way to starting a new career in the medical interpreting field.

Reina soon was hired by a local hospital. The pay wasn't great or steady, but she loved the job. She was also supplementing her income with teaching engagements and private clients: actors, lawyers and spouses from all walks of life frustrated by not being able to communicate with their Latinx partners.

Six months into working in hospitals, a friend she hadn't spoken to in years reconnected with her and told her she was also working as a medical interpreter and teaching Spanish at a college. She went on to tell her about agencies that employed interpreters and about working in immigration courts. That's how she started doing interpretation for immigration courts. After a telephonic test with one of the agencies, she was on her own, wandering around in the courts, stumbling with concepts, phrases and words that didn't make sense to her. She'd thought the telephonic test had prepared her for what was coming. It had not.

That story is quite familiar for the new interpreter. You will hear the same story from interpreters in every state you visit. The reality is that the beginning interpreter lacks training and study materials to start doing the complex job of interpreting in immigration courts. And that was one of the many reasons why this book was conceived.

So, are you a natural-born interpreter or do you need a little push to start studying to become one? If you are thinking about jumping into the world of interpreting, may you find inspiration in this book. Let's walk you through the steps to becoming a beginner interpreter in the professional world.

How to use this manual

The chapter "Theory vs. Reality" will give you concrete information about what the life of an interpreter is like and how you might fit into the world of interpreting for immigration courts. Using real-world examples, the manual will show you who the players are in this world and the rigor, seriousness and high standards they bring to their work, so that you can emulate them from the beginning.

If this book can leave you with one message, it's that—no matter what—you *can* become an interpreter. This manual also will explain in detail how you can start now without having to take thousands of courses to do the job. It'll provide you with solid tips on how to place yourself in a high-demand position and how to polish your skills as a beginner. You'll also learn the importance of properly using standard courtroom equipment to avoid pitfalls from the get-go.

Starting with "Practice Lesson #1: Master Calendar Hearings," you'll notice words in **bold** type throughout this manual. The bold type indicates slang words and colloquialisms. You can find the meanings of those words in the glossary at the back of this book. You will also find footnotes providing you with the sources of definitions and supplemental information in order to give you the opportunity to enhance your reading on the topics in question.

The first practice lesson will define the *master calendar hearing* and cover aspects of what to expect. It will also give you vignettes of court exchanges among the immigration judge, the respondent and the attorneys. *Respondent* is the term used to refer to the noncitizen immigrant who is in removal proceedings. You'll learn that during these sessions you're not alone in court; in immigration courtrooms you'll meet interpreters of multiple languages and nationalities as well as attorneys, clerks, security guards, respondents and respondents' families. This chapter will teach you techniques and give you tools to begin working in master calendar sessions successfully. These lessons will give you the chance to practice using exercises that illustrate how to use different modes of interpretation during master calendar.

The section "Master Calendar Hearings in Immigration Courts and Detention Centers" covers master calendar sessions. You'll also find information about the work shifts and challenges of working in detention centers. Are you up for the task of working in detention centers? Do you have what it takes to work in confined locations? This section will help you to find the answers.

The vignettes provided in this chapter are designed for beginners. They are preceded by instructions and descriptions of settings based on situations you'll encounter in court.

"Practice Lesson #2: Individual Hearings" will provide definitions and examples for you to practice. This lesson will delineate strategies and techniques for how to prepare for your first hearing.

The chapter titled "Practice Lesson #3: An Inside Look at 'The Hearing'" will prepare you for "Practice Lesson #4: 'The Hearing.'" This inside look will help you understand all the elements of a typical asylum hearing, the parts involved as well as the strategies and methods used by the respondent's attorneys and assistant chief counsels. You'll find tips and guidance for preparing for the final exercise, "The Hearing," where you'll practice interpreting only direct and cross-examination by the judge and attorneys.

The chapter titled "Asylum Hearing Practice Lesson: 'The Hearing'" is a fictionalized multilingual asylum hearing. Note that it is abridged and is not a full-fledged case.

Also note that "The Hearing" exercise is designed for the beginning interpreter. Please understand that in a real case, it's possible that the respondent will use more intricate language than you'll encounter here when it comes to the use of slang, regionalisms or colloquialisms of the region in question. For the purposes of preparing the beginning interpreter, the manual balances the load of those gyrations of language so that they will not be too cumbersome.

This is an exercise that you and your partner, classmates or even a lawyer friend can use to practice the consecutive or simultaneous interpretation modes.

"The Hearing" is divided into blocks for easy interpretation, topic focus and easy handling of the task at hand. In the instructions, you'll see the parts involved. In the settings, you'll see two situations labeled *A* and *B*.

Feel free to consult your bilingual dictionary during the exercise.

Disclaimer: This manual is not intended, nor should it be construed in any way, as legal advice.

Theory vs. Reality

Who becomes an immigration interpreter?

You will probably have friends, spouses or relatives who've been interpreting all their lives, even as kids, for a parent or *abuelos*; this is a daily occurrence in every town, pueblo and hamlet of America. Interpreters, for the most part, are immigrants to this country and come from a diverse ethnic background.

Now, whom would you see in courts working as interpreters? You'll meet freelance bilingual, trilingual and polylingual individuals. Among them are:

> college language professors and
> schoolteachers
>
> flight attendants on layover
>
> housewives
>
> missionaries
>
> lawyers, students of law and paralegals
>
> retirees
>
> small-business owners
>
> per diem estate and federal interpreters
> supplementing their income, some retired
>
> certified medical interpreters

translators

real estate agents and others who work in
commission-based jobs

actors, dancers, filmmakers and visual artists

students paying their way through college

But if you don't fall into any of these categories, don't
let it dissuade you; immigrants with limited English language
proficiency need you.

Polylingual interpreters are a coveted group. For
instance, at one point you will meet and work with Spanish-
speaking interpreters from Central America whose knowledge of
languages is within the Mayan cluster of tongues, such as Maya
K'iche', Q'anjob'al and Mam.

If you are someone from Guatemala who speaks Maya
K'iche' in addition to Spanish, you have a job in immigration
court. Imagine having a respondent whose main language is
Maya K'iche' and who has limited knowledge of Spanish. How
do you interpret for this person? In cases like this, the
immigration judge will request, at the petition of the respondent,
two interpreters, one with knowledge of Spanish and Maya

K'iche' and a second interpreter with fluency in Spanish and English. This is called *relay interpreting.*

This is how it works: There would be two interpreters. You sit next to a colleague who speaks Maya K'iche' and Spanish who is interpreting for a Maya K'iche' family from Guatemala. So, you receive the utterance in Spanish and your job is to relay it in English for the parties present. When the immigration judge, the attorneys, or the witnesses speak in English, your job is to interpret that utterance into Spanish and your colleague will then relay it in Maya K'iche' for the family.

So, it's important for you to establish a solid working relationship with all interpreters because at one point or another, you'll need to work together to achieve the common goal of interpreting. And this working relationship comes as a great help when you are called upon to perform relay interpreting, which may happen even as a new interpreter.

Beginner's luck

It sometimes happens that the first cases you face are "easy," whether because a case is just a simple master calendar or a short application for voluntary departure case or because your cases get adjourned minutes after they began. You'll rock it and feel happy about your performance. Nothing wrong with that. Unfortunately, that isn't the experience of most interpreters and some want to quit after their first full hearing.

Travel cases: you might as well have fun!

Besides freelance interpreters, the courts employ full-time personnel. Some bigger courts in large cities have full-time interpreters on staff, and some detention centers do as well. Providing coverage for permanent staff can give you an opportunity to travel. Travel cases in immigration are those where you travel outside of your region to cover for permanent staff interpreters who are on leave of absence or vacation, or for courts that don't have enough interpreters, or have a high volume of cases or last-minute emergencies. This is a great way to practice your skills as a novice interpreter, gain experience you need and learn from a vast array of cases, interpreters, IJs and attorneys.

Rather than complaining about not having enough assignments, ask to take some travel cases. But be mindful: if you are assigned to and end up taking a lot of those cases, it could take a toll on your health or family. Don't overdo it!

On the flip side, travel cases are a wonderful way to get to know the nation: to watch local performances, listen to local bands and see the best natural, architectural and historic attractions that each city offers. What about catching a traveling Broadway show at a discount at a local theater with ample, comfortable seats? Priceless! Sometimes that's a better experience than going to New York and watching a show in a cramped seat on Broadway or off-off-Broadway. What about sampling the best barbecues and seafood you can imagine in Dallas, Houston and Pearsall, Texas, and listening to soulful blues on Beale Street in downtown Memphis? If you live with frigid winters, you might like to visit the New Orleans, Miami or even Hawaii courts. You'll find an excuse to soak in the crystalline waters of warm beaches, even during wintertime.

These are just a few of the advantages of interpreting nationwide. But enough about the perks, as this isn't a travel guidebook!

Courtroom equipment: headsets and microphones

One important factor to remember is that all information exchanged in court is digitally recorded; you won't see a stenographer. You'll have a monitor set to which you attach a headset with a lapel microphone for yourself, used so you can speak simultaneously to as many as three people. Usually, courts keep available up to three more monitors and headsets for the respondent(s) and their family members. In addition, you'll have a microphone on your desk that records your voice and you'll see microphones hanging from the ceiling that record any noise in the courtroom. This is one reason why court officers, clerks and IJs constantly ask respondents and visitors in the room to remain quiet and to turn off their devices while proceedings are conducted.

Tip!

Always leave the monitor plugged in and charging. Be considerate! Take care of your fellow interpreter who will use it next. Fully charged equipment helps guarantee a smooth transition from session to session.

Lesson Learned

The first time Ximena had to work for an extremely well-known demanding immigration judge, she wanted to make a good impression. She came into the courtroom and tested all the monitors, and they all seemed to be working fine. But a few minutes into the hearing, the monitor went silent. Ximena wanted to die. It took her by surprise; after all, she was certain she'd checked the monitors. It was her fault: She didn't check the *charge* in the monitors, and in that case the batteries in the monitor were defective.

Before the start of any case, make sure you check your equipment and verify it has enough charge before you commence your session. If there are any problems, inform the clerk right away so you don't make the person you're interpreting for nervous or make yourself look unprepared—or like a rookie—especially if it is your first appearance.

If for some reason any of the monitors are not fully charged, plug them in or ask the clerk for new batteries.

Troubleshooting:

Check all monitors' batteries. Sometimes they use rechargeable ones.

Make sure all the monitors are working. Some may be defective or overused. Did the interpreter who worked before you neglect to charge the monitors? Always double-check before your session that everything is working for your case!

Before each session, check the sound system. First, make sure attorneys for the respondents can hear you well through the headsets and understand you in English. Then, with the attorney's permission, make sure the respondent hears you through the headsets.

Muted monitor? If they can't hear you, sometimes it's simply that your monitor has been muted to avoid recording background noise coming from your desk.

Wrong frequency? Synchronize monitors to the same frequency. Your monitor must be on the same frequency as the monitors of respondents and/or their families.

Prep makes perfect: lawyers and judges are well-prepared!

José Gregorio remembers auditioning for an experimental production of the opera *Carmen*, in which—luckily for him—he got the lead role, *Don José*. He noticed that during the first day of rehearsals some of the singers were law students. They all told him the reason they were in that theater opera project was because some of their teachers had recommended they take acting and voice lessons to prepare them for the real fight in court. Why don't you as well?

It just so happens that many attorneys and judges, on top of all their knowledge of legal lingo, are also avid readers. Some—especially judges—often use words, phrases and passages from Shakespeare and other canonical works of English and American literature.[1]

So, to put this in context, let's say that during a hearing an attorney or the IJ says, "Is this a dagger which I see before me, the handle toward my hand?" If you don't know this line

---

[1] The Shakespeare Theatre Company produced a "mock trial" series production of *Twelfth Night* that's lots of fun and illustrates what this passage is trying to forewarn you about. See www.shakespearetheatre.org.

from *Macbeth*, what would you do? Don't reach for your glossary or dictionary! You're not supposed to know every proverb, joke and Shakespearean citation by heart. Simply say, "Your Honor, the interpreter needs clarification." Or even use the spelling-bee question: "Can you use that in a sentence or provide the interpreter with an example?"

So be mindful that lawyers and judges are trained to speak in the highest registers, which means you should be an educated speaker as well.

Remember!

A good interpreter is one with knowledge of a wide array of topics and speaking registers from the lowest, most casual to the highest, most formal.

Tip!

Strive for acquiring lots of knowledge and widening your register! For most people, this is ever a work in progress.

Practice Lesson #1: Master Calendar Hearings

Definitions:

Master Calendar hearings are the hearings that take place in a noncitizen's case before a case is scheduled for a final hearing, also known as the individual hearing. A wide variety of matters is addressed during master calendar hearings, including pleadings, presentation of evidence, admission or exclusion of evidence, motions, determination of eligibility for relief from removal, filing of applications for relief, advisals regarding biometrics appointments, scheduling, pretrial conferences, issuance of intermediary orders, voluntary departure prior to the conclusion of removal proceedings, and, in certain instances, the issuance of removal orders.[2]

Respondent is the term used to refer to the noncitizen immigrant who is in removal proceedings.

The term "noncitizen" is used in lieu of "alien" and includes those persons who are not U.S. citizens or nationals, such as nonimmigrants, immigrants, lawful permanent residents, asylees, refugees, and undocumented noncitizens.[3]

---

[2] Immigration Trial Handbook. Maria Baldini-Potermin. Chapter 5, Master Calendar Hearing. § 5:1 Generally and new docketing priorities. Page 270. (Retrieved on October 5, 2019)

[3] Immigration Trial Handbook. Maria Baldini-Potermin. I. Introduction. §1:2 Inadmissibility and deportability. Page 4. (Retrieved on October 5, 2019)

Charging Document

The document that orders an alien to appear before an Immigration Judge. Immigration Court proceedings begin when the Department of Homeland Security mails or delivers the charging document to the alien and files it with the Immigration Court.[4]

So, here you have examples of definitions that you'll be interpreting for respondents and/or their families.

Also, during master calendar hearings you'll often hear the voice of one or two interpreters over the speakers, interpreting languages other than yours. Sometimes the service of a telephonic interpreter is solicited when there's a scheduling conflict or if the one assigned to the hearing didn't make it for some reason. This way, you can hear how interpreters of different languages interpret.

Tip!

Create your own master calendar diary-glossary.

Having your own master calendar diary-glossary will help you memorize new terminology in context. Putting words

---

[4] Immigration Court Practice Manual. 2018 Edition. Office of the Chief Immigration Judge. Naumchenko, Evgenia (Ed.). Independently published. 2019. Glossary. (Retrieved on September 21, 2020)

or phrases into a real situation will help your retention and your ability to recall terminology when you need it. Master calendar hearings demand *speed* from the interpreter. Thus, focus on practicing your speed in context, especially using simultaneous interpreting.

Word of caution!

When creating diaries or recalling events in court, make sure you don't disclose the names and personal information of those individuals involved. As an interpreter, you must keep the strict confidentiality of the persons whose proceedings you are interpreting and never discuss details of their case with anyone.

What does master calendar mean for you, the new interpreter? The master calendar hearing is a very fast-paced session. A master calendar hearing is a short preliminary hearing. It is akin to an arraignment in criminal cases. A master calendar hearing may take just a few minutes, or it may take half an hour. Again, speed is the key component in this session. First, you must be ready to use primarily the simultaneous mode of interpretation. In addition, you may be asked to sight-translate documents and provide announcements out loud to congregants in the gallery or detainees present in court. You will have to interpret for respondents and their family members who will be sitting at a desk facing the immigration judge with their respondent's attorney or with their qualified non-lawyer accredited representatives.

The consecutive mode of interpretation is also used during master calendar. Usually, toward the end of the master calendar docket, IJs call the pro se, or unrepresented, respondents. This portion of the calendar hearing can be challenging for a new interpreter. The pro se respondent has to answer questions asked by the IJ. In many occasions, the respondent has to answer the same number of questions, if not more, as a lawyer or accredited representative would answer for their clients. Respondents, by the same token, often ask questions, trying to understand the process they are involved in for the purpose of finding a solution to their situation. So, a big responsibility falls on your shoulders to make certain this session runs not only smoothly but also with an extreme degree of accuracy. You could very well be the only person sitting next to that pro se respondent. Without the presence of a bilingual lawyer or family member, no one else can correct a mistake. For instance, the immigration judge could ask the respondent to plead to the charges in the Notice to Appear or charging document (Form I-862) they were served, or the IJ could be qualifying the pro se respondent for voluntary departure by asking her various questions, in which case you'll also have the ICE (government attorney) asking questions of the respondents and addressing the immigration judge. You'll have to interpret any verbal exchanges between the ICE attorney and the immigration judge in the simultaneous mode.

Master calendar sessions usually take place during the morning, and an immigration judge will usually set the afternoon for individual or "merits" hearing. Also, depending on case volume, the master calendar docket could run during the morning and into the early afternoon, although the afternoon sessions are usually reserved for individual hearings.

Remember!

Accuracy is key at all times, but especially so when interpreting for the pro se respondent!

During master calendar sessions you'll have to be ready to use the three modes of interpretation: simultaneous, sight translation and consecutive. You may be called upon to switch from one mode to another during a proceeding. Be prepared!

Tip!

Attend several master calendar sessions before you're scheduled to interpret. Hearings in removal proceedings are generally open to the public.[5]

Master calendar sessions are conducted throughout the day, but they usually happen in the morning starting at eight or eight thirty. Before delving into master calendar interpretation, attend sessions in your language to become familiar with what can be quite demanding proceedings for a new interpreter. On a given day you may find different immigration judges conducting master calendars. It would be helpful to watch how each IJ conducts his sessions and how each treats the same procedure. Take lots of notes and even try to practice whispering while you're in court. Master calendars are very challenging even for the seasoned interpreter. Ask experienced interpreters for any

---

[5] Immigration Court Practice Manual. 2018 Edition. Office of the Chief Immigration Judge. Naumchenko, Evgenia (Ed.). Independently published. 2019. Chapter 4.9 Public Access (a) General Public. (i) Hearings. (Retrieved on October 15, 2019)

scripts, glossaries or ideas that would enable you to improve in speed and accuracy. Most IJs like to finish their masters fast, so be prepared. Anticipate! Study, learn and memorize all the advisals, forms and sequences of events of as many IJs you can so that when you go to an unknown IJ, you pretty much know all possible "variations of the theme."

In a given master calendar hearing you could interpret for fifty-plus people. So be hydrated! As described above, you'll have your own monitor with a microphone and two or three monitors with headphones for respondents and their families. If the equipment doesn't work for any reason, ask the IJ if you can position yourself behind the respondents and their families so you can interpret simultaneously, although you may encounter IJs who ask you to interpret the entire calendar in the consecutive mode.

Master calendars can be organized or chaotic. In some courts you'll see flocks of people coming in and out, as well as respondents' attorneys running in and yelling out the names of clients they're trying to locate, which can be a distraction for the interpreter. So, you'll need to stay focused!

Tip!

Ask the IJ for permission to take some of the immigration forms in the waiting area or on counsel's tables so you can become familiar with them. Then if you are asked to sight-translate, you'll have a leg up in the game.

Master calendar hearings: shifts

While master calendar sessions usually start as early as eight o'clock, there are IJs who start at eight thirty, nine or nine thirty, with a break between sessions before finally breaking for lunch at noon. Some sessions start even later, and some sessions finish earlier than noon.

You'll find more about shifts in "Practice Lesson #2: Individual Hearings."

Tip!

Memorize abbreviations used in court to speed up your interpretation.

Common abbreviations

For both master calendar and individual hearings, abbreviations are used often, especially by the IJ and attorneys. Here are some of the most common.

A#: alien registration number

ACC: assistant chief counsel

BIA: Board of Immigration Appeals

CIMT: crime involving moral turpitude

GMC: good moral character

ICE: U.S. Immigration and Customs Enforcement

IJ: immigration judge

LPR: lawful permanent resident

MC: master calendar

NTA: Notice to Appear (Form I-862)

USCIS: U.S. Citizen and Immigration Services

VD: voluntary departure

Master calendar hearings at detention and transitional centers

Before Valentina came to work in a detention center, obviously she didn't know what to expect. It felt intriguing for her. Would there be IJs, attorneys, respondents and their families inside the courtroom? She had no idea! So here are some of the possibilities you can expect in detention centers.

Obviously, expect an immigration judge, a Department of Homeland Security Immigration and Customs Enforcement (DHS-ICE) assistant chief counsel (or trial attorney—TA), security guard(s), clerk(s), inmate-respondent(s) pro se or with their lawyer(s) to be in the courtroom or appear by televideo. Some detention centers allow family members to attend hearings because sometimes they are questioned during those hearings. In other facilities, those allowed in the courtroom included the detainee-respondent(s), along with one ICE agent present in the office and the IJ and DHS assistant chief counsel attending remotely by televideo.

There may be many instances when you'll be asked to cover for sick staff interpreters or for someone on vacation or who had a last-minute emergency. In most of those instances you will end up going to locations that are new to you. If you're sent to an unfamiliar site, you don't know what to expect, and you may find there's no fellow interpreter around you can ask. You won't know whether you'll be allowed to bring in your personal items, laptop, phone, water bottle, food and other items you otherwise may be allowed to bring into a familiar immigration court.

Now, this is a critical point, isn't it? You're unaware not only of the working conditions of the new location but also of the culture and the common practice of that court, particularly of the presiding IJ. The normal thing to do is rely on experience. So, there you go all confident, thinking you know it all (I've been there, done that), and you'll think: What could go wrong? Since you've interpreted for a number of master calendar hearings, you'll just rely on past experience.

Then you'll be thrown into the unknown and—*boom!*— the new IJ throws you a curveball. The proceedings are a little different from what you are used to or the IJ asks something new of you. For instance, this IJ asks you to spell proper names, slang words—you name it! And you're thinking, *I've never been asked to spell anything, and my glossaries and dictionaries are on my phone.*

For that reason, you should always be prepared for any contingency. Bring paper glossaries to a new location. Bring your dictionaries. Don't expect to be allowed to bring your smart phone or laptop. Don't rely on your memory, either!

Valentina lives in New Orleans and she's used to traveling for work to courts in Dallas, Texas and Orlando, Florida. Once, she was in a Texas court covering for a staff interpreter, and on a Friday afternoon she got a call to go to Las Vegas the following Sunday. She'd never been to Las Vegas and she was excited. But she ended up going to a detention center in the middle of the arid desert. She stayed that night in a motel in an isolated area. There was only a gas station and a bus stop across from it—nothing else! On Monday morning, she asked at the front desk how to get to her destination using public transportation. She always likes to get around a place like the locals do (by bus or on foot), but since it was her first time there, she wanted to be extra careful and learn her way around without mistakes. She also always leaves an hour before the start of the hearing to get to the location.

That wasn't possible in this case. The locals drove and the public bus was unreliable. It was also like a ghost town; even though it was Monday, nothing was open at 5:30 a.m. Finally, Valentina decided to call an Uber car. The driver, a local retiree, was very accommodating, nice and talkative, and that put her at ease. Then in the middle of the conversation she noticed the driver became confused and hesitant. She had taken the wrong turn. But since she'd left the motel with plenty of time, she still reached her destination early. She waited for half an hour outside of the facility. It was nippy, and she was dying to go to the bathroom. It was eight o'clock and the main window was still closed. Someone else, not her, was late.

Once the detention-center personnel opened the window, Valentina identified herself, so she could get in to prepare, put on makeup and go to the bathroom. Of course, they weren't familiar with her, so the security screening took longer, as is the norm in such situations, especially in detention centers. Always factor in that extra time before your hearings.

Next, she found out she was covering vacation for one of the regular interpreters. After all the formalities with identification, she went through a series of security checkpoints and doors, then finally into a room where the officer in charge asked her to sit in front facing a sizable television set. She said to herself, *Okay, why did they bother bringing me all the way here? I could have done this anywhere.*

The space wasn't well-proportioned and had very high ceilings. Valentina kept asking herself, *Don't they have a smaller space for the person I'm interpreting for?* Well, to her surprise, more than fifty inmates in orange garments marched in, ready to face the immigration judge on a huge television screen. Only one ICE agent, who sat in the back of the room, served as both security and secretary to the IJ. One after the other, inmates-respondents came forward and sat next to her, both of them facing the IJ on the large screen. Valentina never saw the DHS assistant chief counsel, only heard her voice occasionally. She didn't have access to a computer, laptop or cell phone—only her glossary, dictionary, pad and pencil—and sat side by side with anxious inmates, most of whom ended up taking orders of removal for their native countries rather than remaining detained.

There are tough considerations to keep in mind when it comes to working in detention centers. Are you willing to work under the tremendous pressure you may feel when so many security doors have closed behind you? Are you willing to stay for hours at a time in an enclosed room—sometimes larger rooms, other times tiny rooms where inmates with extensive rap sheets sit elbow to elbow with you, with just one guard present? The purpose of this line of thinking is not to scare you away from this work, but to make you sure you know what you'll be up against, because your mental stability and capability of performing your job will determine another person's future. Don't wait until you're inside a detention center to decide whether this is the type of work you want to do. It's very important for you to feel comfortable doing this job.

Once Valentina finished the master calendar session that morning, it was time to process and fax the voucher to get paid. The fax machine was located on a raised island of sorts with desks and computers. Cells surrounded the raised island. The constant shouting and screaming from the cells was deafening and nerve-racking, and she couldn't escape from it. When the fax wouldn't go through for some unfortunate reason, she had to endure the horrific sounds of desperate inmates. It was midday on a beautiful sunny day, but when she finally reached her hotel in downtown Vegas, ready to have lunch in the casinos, she could still hear the screaming and yelling she'd heard that morning. That was Valentina's first trip to Las Vegas.

Instructions for Vignette 1a

Exercise: interpreting from a detention center at a master calendar session

Instructions: For each setting (A) and (B), record all the parts of the dialogue: immigration judge (IJ), assistant chief counsel (ACC) and respondent (R). Interpret each using the appropriate mode.

Settings:

>(A) You, the interpreter, are sitting at the interpreter's booth with a headset on. You're sitting on the IJ's right side and diagonally across from the ACC's desk twenty feet away. The inmate appears pro se, sitting toward the left side of the IJ, twenty-five feet away from you. A security guard is next to him.

>(B) You, the interpreter, are sitting to the right of the respondent. The IJ and ACC appear remotely on a television screen. A respondent's attorney is appearing over the phone. There is an ICE security officer with you and the inmate in the room.

Vignette 1a to interpret:

The immigration judge turns on the recording equipment at the beginning of the master calendar hearing. The hearing is recorded except for off-the-record discussions.[6]

IJ: *We're now on the record. This is a removal proceeding, on file number A 881-957-309, in the case of Juan López. Today is January third of 2020, approximately 9:30 a.m. Good morning, sir. Raise your right hand. Do you swear under the penalty of perjury that the testimony you're about to give shall be the truth, all the truth and nothing but the truth?*

R: Lo juro. Será la verdad, su señoría.

IJ: *Say your name and date of birth for the record, sir?*

R: Me llamo Juan López. Nací el trece de agosto, señorita...

(R looks at the interpreter.)

R: ¿El año? 1991.

(R looks at the interpreter.)

R: El juez tiene mi partida de nacimiento, señorita intérprete.

---

[6] Immigration Court Practice Manual. 2018 Edition. Office of the Chief Immigration Judge. Naumchenko, Evgenia (Ed.). Independently published. 2019. Chapter 4.15. Master Calendar Hearing. (f) Opening of a master calendar hearing. (Retrieved on October 5, 2019)

IJ: *Sir, did you have the chance to speak to a lawyer or legal aid representative in this area?*

R: No, su señoría, pero con el favor de dios así lo haré.

IJ: *Mr. López, did you receive the golden aid list of free representatives?*

R: Así es, su señoría… sí, y hablé con un notario amigo de mi cuñada.

IJ: *Did you talk to Catholic Charities of Northern Nevada or Legal Aid Services, Mr. López?*

R: No, su señoría... Como le dije al *officer*... hablé con Jesús, el notario amigo de la esposa de mi hermano menor. Él vive en *Utah*. Él tiene su oficinita en *Logan*, en la *568 Quarter Nickel Dime Drive*.

IJ: *Thank you, Mr. López. Sir, you're charged with being in this country illegally. I am going to read the charges and you will admit or deny the charges contained in the Notice to Appear, Form I-862. The NTA alleges that you are not a citizen of the United States. You are a citizen and native of Mexico. That you entered the United States without being inspected or paroled by an immigration officer.*

(Long pause. The sound becomes muted. The IJ shuffles several papers, unmutes the microphone and directs his attention to the respondent.)

IJ: *Sir, when you entered the United States you had a visa border card that allowed you to remain in this country for five days and within twenty-five miles. But then you passed the twenty-five miles and ended up in Buenos Aires.*

R: ¿Buenos Aires?

IJ: *Yes, you ended up in Buenos Aires National Wildlife Refuge, Sasabe, in the United States territory. Isn't that true, Mr. López?*

R: ¡Así es! Sí, sí, sí, yo estoy de acuerdo con todo eso.

IJ: *Sir, I am then going to sustain the charge on the NTA. You are allowed to designate a country of removal if deportation becomes necessary. Would you like to designate a country?*

R: ¡No! no, no, su señoría... yo no quiero regresar a ningún país... ¡Aquí me quedo!

IJ: *Sir, the assistant chief counsel in the Form I-213, Record of Deportable/Inadmissable Alien, notes that you were charged with illegal possession of marijuana, possession of methamphetamine and possession of a small quantity of cocaine and that you were convicted and sentenced in Utah in three different dockets for those crimes. Do you remember what you were sentenced for, Mr. López?*

R: Yo sí sé que el cargo por marihuana me lo quitaron, ese casito se selló... me informó el defensor público. El fiscal no pudo probarme nada, el cargo se eliminó y lo sellaron.

IJ: *And what about the other dockets? Were they disposed of?*

R: Son casos pendientes, señor juez.

IJ: *How did ICE locate you, sir?*

R: ¿Qué dijo él?

(R stares at the interpreter, then immediately answers the question without needing repetition.)

R: ¡Ah! este, este... Iba en mi bicicleta por la acera y un policía me detuvo, me paró.

IJ: *You were riding your bike on the sidewalk and the police stopped you and apprehended you?*

R: ¡Aha! ¡Aha! sí, su señoría.

IJ: *I also see that you were charged by the Nevada County Jail on July 26 for possession of drug paraphernalia. Isn't that correct, sir?*

R: ¡Aha! ¡Aha! así es pues.

IJ: *Do you have parents who are citizens of the United States?*

R: ¡No, señor! No, no. ¿Yo? No.

IJ: *Do you have children born in the U.S.?*

R: ¿Niños? No, no tengo **chavos**.

IJ: *So, sir, the charges I just mentioned disqualify you to obtain what is called cancellation of removal.*

R: ¿Qué es eso? ¿Me repite? Diga usted, por favor.

IJ: *Cancellation of removal application for certain non-permanent residents—sir. Now the only choice you have left is asylum.*

R: Bueno, bueno, ya me habían dicho... ¿me repite la historia, señorita?

IJ: *Are you afraid to return to Mexico?*

R: ¡Añil!

IJ: *Then I'll allow you to apply for asylum. Now officer PM will give you the proper paperwork so you can apply for that relief. Okay?*

R: Y ¿si quiero irme a mi país?

IJ: *Would you like to be deported, Mr. López?*

R: Y ¿me pudieran decir a qué ciudad me mandarían deportado, por favor?

IJ: *Talk to an officer from ICE in your facility. They'll know better than me.*

PM: *They're now being sent to main cities. First, they're sent to a holding point in Arizona, and from there they'll be sent to selected points.*

Tip!

Always interpret in the first person. For example: "I am Margarita" or "I am Ángel." Remember that you are the mouth and ears of every respondent you interpret for! You become that person. Never say, "She's Margarita," or, "He's Ángel."

Tip!

Read every handout, form and brochure you can find in court.

Almost every court keeps handouts, forms and paper packets explaining the types of benefits against deportation, waiver forms, applications for relief, the appeal process and other important instructions. Read them, research unknown words and ask questions before you interpret for a master calendar session. Those documents are a great source of information and key vocabulary that you will use during master calendar and some individual hearings when you provide instructions to respondents and their families.

Instructions for Vignette 1b:

Exercise: remote interpreting by videoconferencing

Instructions: Record all parts: IJ, ACC, R. Interpret using the consecutive mode.

Setting: The IJ is presiding in a court inside a detention center. Sitting at the DHS desk is the assistant chief counsel with a supervisor. Also in court are a security guard and you, the interpreter. You are sitting at the interpreter's desk to the left of the IJ. The assistant chief counsel is seated diagonally from you. The detainee-respondent appears remotely on a TV set. The IJ presiding over the case is in the middle of a hearing addressing charges contained in the document Form I-213, Record of Deportable/Inadmissible Alien, previously provided to the respondent by the assistant chief counsel.

Vignette 1b to interpret:

IJ: *Sir, are you aware that you have been charged and convicted for using drug paraphernalia in Miami, Florida?*

R: En 2012, su señoría… Mi abogado me obligó a declararme culpable. Mi abogado así me aconsejó. Yo solo visitaba el laboratorio y trabajaba barriendo allí, raras veces, una que otra vez por semana... Yo incluso hice *community service for that conviction, Your Honor.*

IJ: *You were apprehended in Idaho, right?*

R: *In Utah. No, I am sorry.* ¿cómo dijo usted?

IJ: *No, sir, in Idaho.*

R: Sí, sí, esta última vez fue *in Idaho. I blew through the stop sign and boom!*

IJ: *Do you have family in the U.S., sir?*

R: Toda mi familia vive aquí en los Estados Unidos y... en Miami, en Orlando, por aquí en San Francisco también. A mí no me queda nadie en *Cuba, Your Honor.*

IJ: *Then you may be able to apply for cancellation of removal.*

R: ¿Cancelación de qué? ¿Una expulsión?

IJ: *Yes, sir! Cancellation of removal. Now, sir, please first listen. If you win your case, you can go home and report every _____ [number of days].*

R: *I see. I see. I understand everything.*

IJ: *What would you like to do, sir? Would you like time to consult a free lawyer?*

R: Voy a pelear, voy a aplicar por *cancellation,* hablaré con un *attorney, Your Honor.*

IJ: *Now, it'll take _____ [number of days] to give you a hearing day and from thirty to ninety days to release you.*

R: No, no, no, yo no quiero pasar más tiempo en este demonio de cárcel.

IJ: *Then I'm signing an order of deportation to your home country of Cuba. Officer PM will give you the order.*

R: *When would I be deported?*

Tip!

If you feel stressed out, ask for a break! The job of interpreting can be extremely demanding and stressful. You can imagine the frustration and desperation that respondents experience. Maintain your cool and make sure your performance is not tarnished by any obstacles.

Remotely held master calendar hearings by televideo at detention centers—bond and bond redetermination hearings

There are courts that hold master calendar hearings with detained respondents, and once those hearings finish, they move to remote hearings by televideo.

The master calendar consists of two sections: the preliminary matters master calendar and the bond hearing or bond redetermination hearing. You should be prepared to interpret for both hearings.

When respondents are in the courtroom, you have to be prepared to interpret either simultaneously or consecutively, depending on the IJ's preference. Once the respondent-inmates appear on the screen, you'll be asked to interpret in the consecutive mode.

During such hearings, there's sometimes a twist with a voluntary departure or an order of removal. So, beware: these hearings are expected to be short and to the point, but sometimes they can become lengthy and complicated. You'll find yourself having to interpret lots of questions from the DHS assistant chief counsel qualifying the respondent for the voluntary departure relief, going through lengthy rap sheets or interpreting testimony given by relatives of the respondents.

Tip!

Knowledge of criminal vocabulary comes in handy during these hearings.

In some courts, master calendar sessions and bond determination hearings are a common routine, where hearings are done in person and/or remotely by televideo. You may have a group of detainees brought from a detention center or a transitional or penal facility. Attorneys for respondent(s), accredited representatives and relatives of the detainees come into the court as well. Some attorneys will show up telephonically. The order of in-person and televideo sessions from a remote detention center may vary.

Instructions for Vignette 1c:

Exercise: interpreting for a bond redetermination hearing at a master calendar session in a detention center

Instructions: For each setting, record all the parts of the dialogue and interpret in the consecutive mode first.

Settings:

> (A) Imagine that the R (detainee-respondent) is sitting next to you. The IJ and ACC are at a remote location. You will see the IJ on a screen, but you'll only hear the ACC and never be able to see her.

> (B) Imagine that the R (detainee-respondent) is at a remote location. You're sitting in the interpreter's booth in a courtroom to the right of the IJ. The ACC is sitting at her desk diagonally from you and at a lower level.

Vignette 1c to interpret:

After some preliminary matters are dealt with and the IJ asks questions, the D (respondent's attorney)—here, Mr. Cohn—presents his argument about bond.

D: *Your Honor, I am requesting a seven hundred and fifty-dollar bond for Mr. Ramos. My client has significant ties in his community. He lives with his fiancée, who happens to be the mother and stepmother of his two children: Ms. Vallesteros, who is in the gallery here today, Your Honor. He has lived there in Upper Fell's Point for five years, since he came to the U.S. He participates in the activities of his church, the Spanish Seventh-day Adventist Church. Mr. Ramos has two U.S.-citizen children. He is not a flight risk. He has worked for Flowers and Prickles Landscaping for at least a year. He's been in compliance with probation and the drug and alcohol treatment program that was mandated by the Circuit Court for Baltimore City, where Mr. Ramos was detained. His rap sheet shows one conviction only for a DUI and driving without insurance and registration. He is able and willing to post bond for the amount of seven hundred and fifty dollars, Your Honor.*

ACC: *Mr. Cohn, looking at the respondent's criminal history chart,*[7] *I see several arrests on top of the one you mentioned. I am now referring to Tab F, pages eleven to thirteen. This is a charge for possession of an open container in Las Vegas, Nevada, on January 28, 2019. The disposition in this case was that your client pleaded guilty. Also, if you look at Tab G, page fourteen, there's a charge for disorderly conduct in Adams County, Idaho, on February of the same year.*

(ACC pauses and continues reading silently from the chart.)

IJ: *Anything else, Ms. Petrov?*

ACC: *Well, if you turn to Tab H on pages fifteen to seventeen, I see charges for trespassing and damaging property in Twins Falls County, Idaho, in August of 2018. Your Honor, Mr. Ramos has an extensive rap sheet, and on top of that, there is a conviction for possession of drug paraphernalia inside a motor vehicle—*

D: *Where do you see that charge, Ms. Petrov?*

ACC: *The court docket is 53399. Tab Q—*

(D interrupts ACC.)

---

[7] Immigration Court Practice Manual. 2018 Edition. Office of the Chief Immigration Judge. Naumchenko, Evgenia (Ed.). Independently published. 2019. Appendix O. Sample Criminal History Chart. (Retrieved on October 15, 2019)

D: *I apologize, Your Honor. I wasn't aware of those charges. But you'll agree with me that those crimes don't rise to the level of CIMT.*

IJ: *What level of bond do you propose, Ms. Petrov, and why?*

Pleading for charges of removability during master calendar hearings

In most immigration courts, the respondent's attorneys plead simply using the NTA document, Form I-862. In other immigration courts, you will see the IJ ask respondents' attorneys to plead using a form that can be found at the United States Department of Justice website by searching for "Immigration Court Practice Manual" and looking for Appendix M—Sample Oral Pleading. Attorneys use this form as a guide and draw information and language from the NTA. You may see this way of pleading in both regular immigration courts and detention centers. In this instance, you get a copy of the oral pleading form that the respondent's attorney is using and you will follow along as the attorney reads it and adds information from the NTA. Don't let this take you by surprise! You can ask in advance to read and review a blank oral pleading form.

In general, most respondent's attorneys follow the pleading document closely and read it at full speed. They have the document in front of them, and they just fill in the blanks as they go using the NTA. And boy, they go fast! The advantage of it is that you'll have the same document in front of you that the respondent's attorney will be using, but still, practice in anticipation. Note that the document is in a standard form containing blanks related to biometric and other information specific to the client and information drawn from the NTA Form I-862, which will be different each time.

Again, not all courts follow this format, but it will be a good practice for you anyway. Also imagine interpreting for a pro se respondent and that the IJ requests that the respondent plead to the NTA. Then either you'll have to sight-translate that document or you'll be asked to follow along reading from your copy simultaneously with the IJ.

Tip!

Prepare way in advance so you are familiar with the content and sequence of the blank oral pleading form.

Instructions for Vignette 1d:

Exercise: interpreting during pleading for charges of removability during master calendar hearing

Instructions: For this exercise, you will need two documents: (1) the sample oral pleading document that you can find at the United States Department of Justice website by searching for "Immigration Court Practice Manual" and looking for Appendix M—Sample Oral Pleading and (2) an NTA Form I-862. A sample of a blank NTA can be found in the Justice Department website at https://www.justice.gov/eoir/dhs-notice-appear-form-i-862. In order to complete the NTA Form I-862, please use the following information:

Respondent: Ms. Rodríguez

Address: 3056 Dollar Nickel Dime Drive Houston, Texas 77027

Possible charges alleged by the Department of Homeland Security:

1. You are not a citizen or national of the United States

2. You are a native of Argentina and a citizen of Argentina

3. You entered in the United States at or near McAllen, Texas on or about December 31, 2017

4. You were not then admitted or paroled after inspection by an Immigration Officer.

Once you have the blank copy of the NTA Form I-862 in hand, add the information provided. To practice further, make up your own information for the NTA Form I-862.

Then record IJ and D. You'll be interpreting in the simultaneous mode following the recorded sample oral pleading document you just filled out.

Settings:

(A) You, the interpreter, are seated at the interpreter's booth to the right of the IJ facing the ACC. Also present in court are a security officer and, in the gallery, more than twenty respondents with their families and respondent's attorneys.

(B) This time, the respondent and two of her minor children will be seated at their attorney's desk and you will be seated slightly behind the respondents.

Vignette 1d to interpret:

IJ: *Mr. Klein, does your client concede or deny service of the Notice to Appear, Form I-862, dated March 5, 2019?*

D: *Concedes service, Your Honor.*

IJ: *Does your client request or waive an explanation of her rights and obligations in removal proceedings?*

D: *So waived, Your Honor.*

IJ: *Mr. Klein, you can proceed with pleadings using the sample oral pleading form.*

D: *I am ready, Your Honor.*

(D pleads by following the written sample oral pleading form, filling in the blanks that are appropriate to this particular case.)

Remember!

It is the job of the respondent's attorney to fill in those blanks for each pleading.

Tip!

Before attending your first master calendar appearance, practice interpreting the sample oral pleading form many times in simultaneous mode at different speeds.

Voluntary departure (VD) relief during master calendar

Often you will be asked to interpret for a person requesting VD during a master calendar hearing.[8] So become familiar with such relief and the orders dictated by IJs. A voluntary departure order is typically interpreted in the simultaneous mode. If you are interpreting in the consecutive mode, you will take notes reflecting the particulars of the order, the name of the respondent, the amount of time offered to depart, the departure date and any civil penalties imposed. In other words, only take notes on the variations of a typical VD order and make sure you deliver long utterances without having to make the IJ pause in the middle of a sentence. Becoming familiar with VD orders is also helpful when you have to interpret for a pro se respondent with no representation present.

Instructions for Vignette 1e

Exercise: interpreting during a master calendar session for a pro se respondent requesting voluntary departure

---

[8] Immigration Trial Handbook. Maria Baldini-Potermin. § 5:28 Motion for Voluntary Departure. Chapter 5, Master Calendar Hearing. Page 331. (Retrieved on October 5, 2019)

Instructions: Interpret using the consecutive mode. This exercise is divided into two parts, (A) and (B).

(A) The complete text for Part A is included in the vignette below. Record each part: IJ, R, ACC.

(B) To accomplish Part B, you will need the document "NOTICE TO RESPONDENTS GRANTED VOLUNTARY DEPARTURE," which can be downloaded at the justice.gov/eoir website.[9] Note that this document is a standard form containing blanks related mostly to numbers. Again, only worry about standard content that will need to be interpreted each time. It is the job of the IJ to fill in those blanks. Once you have the document in hand, record it and practice.

Setting: Imagine you, the interpreter, are in an immigration court with a room full of lawyers, respondents and family members.

---

[9] NOTICE TO RESPONDENTS GRANTED VOLUNTARY DEPARTURE.
https://www.justice.gov/eoir/page/file/988041/download
(Retrieved on October 15, 2019)

Vignette 1e to interpret:

Part A

After some preliminary matters are dealt with and questions are answered, the respondent requested voluntary departure as her only form of relief.

IJ: *Ms. Quispe, you have requested voluntary departure in lieu of being ordered to be removed from this country. Is that the case, Ms. Quispe?*

R: Sí, señora.

(IJ looks at R and reads aloud.)

IJ: *Now, Ms. Quispe, since you're requesting voluntary departure prior to the completion of your removal proceedings, there are certain criteria that must be met, and I'll explain them to you. You must withdraw any requests for relief and make no additional requests. You must concede removability. You must not have been convicted for an aggravated felony or murder. You must waive appeal of all issues. The immigration judge may impose conditions deemed necessary to ensure timely departure. You may be required to submit travel documents to the DHS. And lastly, there is no requirement of good moral character or any length of physical presence in the U.S.[10]*

---

[10] Immigration Trial Handbook. Maria Baldini-Potermin. § 5:28 Motion for Voluntary Departure. Chapter 5, Master Calendar Hearing. Page 332. (Retrieved on October 5, 2019.)

R: De acuerdo, señora.

IJ: *Now, Ms. Quispe, Ms. Schachtschneider is the attorney who represents Homeland Security and she is going to ask you some questions to qualify you for the relief sought. Do you understand, Ms. Quispe?*

R: ¡Sí, señora!

(IJ interrupts R.)

IJ: *I may also have some questions after the assistant chief counsel direct examination.*

(ACC questions R.)

IJ: *If Ms. Schachtschneider has no objection, I am willing to grant you the relief sought.*

ACC: *The government doesn't object to pre-conclusion voluntary departure, but I'd like to see an ID—a passport or an official identity document, perhaps a travel document from Peru—that bears the name of the respondent as a requisite for her departure, Your Honor—*

(R interrupts ACC.)

R: Tengo mi cédula, señorita. Aquí la tengo y puedo mostrársela si quiere.

IJ: *Ms. Schachtschneider, did you have anything else to say? It seems that Ms. Quispe cut you off.*

ACC: *No, Your Honor, it's okay.*

IJ: *So, is it final for both parties?*

(R replies in loud voice.)

R: Pero juez ¿pudiera salir en tres semanas?

IJ: *Ms. Quispe, as long as you depart the country within the time granted, you'll be fine.*

R: Mi abuelita está muy enferma, su señoría. ¡Entienda usted!

IJ: *So once again, is it final for both parties?*

(R and ACC assent.)

IJ: *I am granting you the privilege of departing voluntarily from the United States of America, Ms. Quispe. I am granting the maximum amount of time that I am allowed under the law, which is _____[number of days]. So, Ms. Quispe, you must depart by or not later than January 1 of 2020. On the contrary, if you don't depart voluntarily from the United States, serious consequences could happen to you, ma'am.*

R: Entiendo, su señoría.

(R stands up and starts walking out.)

Part B

IJ: *Now wait, Ms. Quispe, there're some advisals I must give you before I let you go.*

(IJ reads Notice to Respondents Granted VD.)

Find NOTICE TO RESPONDENTS GRANTED

VOLUNTARY DEPARTURE at

https://www.justice.gov/eoir/page/file/988041/download.

Tip!

Practice VD orders a million times in the sight-translate,

simultaneous and consecutive modes. Why? Because an IJ can

ask you to interpret in any of these modes.

Bond hearing

Definitions:

> In certain circumstances, an alien detained by
> the Department of Homeland Security (DHS)
> can be released from custody upon the
> payment of bond. Initially, the bond is set by
> DHS. Upon the alien's request, an
> Immigration Judge may conduct a "bond
> hearing," in which the Immigration Judge has
> the authority to redetermine the amount of
> bond set by DHS.[11]

On a very hot and dry day during the afternoon,

Santiago walked some fifteen or twenty minutes from a hotel in

downtown Vegas to the building where the individual hearing

---

[11] Immigration Court Practice Manual. 2018 Edition. Office of
the Chief Immigration Judge. Naumchenko, Evgenia (Ed.).
Independently published. 2019. Chapter 9.3 Bond Proceedings.
(Retrieved on October 5, 2019)

was about to take place. That was all the information he had: an address. Once there, he entered the building and went through security and metal detectors on the ground floor. One of the security guards asked him if he had any guns on him. Of course, his answer was no. Wasn't that a clue about the city he was in?

Santiago took an elevator and went to the information window, where he spoke to a clerk. She asked him to wait to be called. He was way ahead of his scheduled time. He didn't want to be admonished by anyone.

There wasn't any cafeteria or Wi-Fi in the small lobby. Minutes later, there was a change of guards. The new guard was tattooed all over and kept changing the TV channel from Fox News to a game show. He seemed to want Santiago to participate with him, so he played along.

At a quarter to twelve he went to the window again. Finally, he was escorted to a different floor. He was placed in a small office with a desk with lots of chairs on both sides. There was also a TV set and a fax machine. The hearing started at 1:05. On the TV screen was the IJ, no clerk and an assistant chief counsel. In minutes, an ICE officer brought in a handcuffed respondent.

Instructions for Vignette 1f:

Exercise: interpreting for a pro se respondent in a bond hearing

Instructions: Record each part: IJ, R, ACC and the ICE agent. Interpret using the consecutive mode.

Setting: You're summoned to appear to interpret for an individual hearing in the afternoon after having interpreted for a master calendar session in the morning at a detention facility for more than fifty detainee-respondents. Needless to say, you are tired. You are escorted to an office where you are seated at a desk with the respondent; in the office, there's an ICE agent as well. The IJ and assistant chief counsel are on a screen, appearing by videoconferencing.

Vignette 1f to interpret:

After the IJ deals with preliminary matters of the hearing, he continues with asking questions.

IJ: *Mr. Castillo, did you receive a certified letter from the LVMPD?*
(R talks while looking at the interpreter.)

R: Disculpe, señor traductor, no sé de qué me habla... Dígame, dígame ¿podré salir bajo fianza?

IJ: *Didn't you obtain a letter from the Las Vegas Metropolitan Police Department, Mr. Castillo? We'll address bond in a second, Mr. Castillo, but let me ask you again: did you get any letter from the LVMPD?*

(R talks while looking at the interpreter.)

R: No recuerdo... no, no creo, no. Nunca me llegó la dichosa carta, señor.

(R lowers his head and utters something unintelligible.)

IJ: *I have information that you suffered battery while in Las Vegas, Nevada. I also have information explaining that you were the victim of spousal abuse back in your hometown of Hermosillo. Also, isn't it true that some members of your ex-wife's family beat you up and forced you to leave town, and because of those reasons you decided to apply for asylum?*

R: *Right, Your Honor!*

IJ: *Did you go to any clinic for the stabbings you suffered—I mean in your hometown, sir?*

R: Una prima me cosió. Mi primita, ella vivía en su casucha a unos kilómetros de **Hermosío**. Un taxista me llevó a su casa. Mi primita, era muy pobre. Ella misma me curó, también me dio remedios caseros y la herida cerró, me hizo una sutura casera, por eso me quedó una cicatriz muy fea. Aquí, aquí... ¿la ve? Se la enseño mejor, digo, si usted quiere verla.

(R pauses and begins opening his shirt, the ICE agent signs at R to stop opening his shirt, R continues opening his shirt.)

IJ: *I see—I can see your scars, Mr. Castillo. Did you bring any report from a doctor or a rehabilitation clinic from your town, Hermosillo?*

R: No, no, pero otro incidente ocurrió mientras andaba yo con los hijos de mi prima.

(R pauses and cries.)

IJ: *What happened? What did they do to you? Did you bring me any documents, Mr. Castillo?*

R: ¡**Nel!** Como le decía, tres jóvenes se me acercaron pidiéndome que les ayudara a vender drogas. Yo me les negué, y con la misma me tiraron a la tierra, golpearon por la espalda y finalmente me patearon. Allí me dejaron tendido.

IJ: *Did you report such a contemptible incident to the police or local authorities?*

R: Claro que lo hice, sí que lo reporté, señores.

IJ: *How come you don't have a report from the police?*

(R talks while looking at the interpreter.)

R: Se extravió el papel, señor... ¿Qué puedo hacer, señor? Este, este... vea usted, la demanda que se hizo se me perdió, se me traspapeló, su señoría.

IJ: *I see in my notes that your uncle went to the police. Why not you,*
Mr. Castillo?

(R looks back at the screen.)

R: Discúlpeme, mi tío fue primero, yo estaba adolorido, enfermo
estaba yo, su señoría. No podía levantarme. Más tarde fui y
colaboré con las autoridades, y metieron preso a los
malhechores, eran unos traficantes.

IJ: *Do you fear to return to Hermosillo, Mexico?*

R: No, no más, su señoría. Es la verdad, es la mera verdad, su
señoría.

IJ: *But you stated in the past that you feared returning to Mexico. Wasn't*
that right, sir?

R: ¡**Añil**, su señoría! Esa fue mi decisión en aquel juicio que tuve,
pero más adelante me platicaron de la U *nonimigrant status visa*, de
la Visa U. Yo fui víctima de un crimen en Los Ángeles, y yo
colaboré con las autoridades, y por eso decidí atenerme a la U.

IJ: *So, let me ask you, Mr. Castillo: why did you want to come to the*
U.S.?

R: Para cumplir mis sueños, **chambear** un poco, comprar
ganado en mi país, y mandar dinero a mi prima. ¡Cumplir el
sueño americano, su señoría!

IJ: *So, you wanted to come to the U.S. for financial reasons, right, Mr. Castillo?*

R: No necesariamente. Fíjese usted, mis tíos, mis tíos que con ellos me crié, ellos me dieron buena educación... ellos estaban bien económicamente... Yo incluso una vez quise venir a estudiar terapia física aquí, vea usted…

(R pauses. R moans, signaling something is wrong with his neck. As R resumes talking, IJ starts talking while looking away from the camera.)

IJ: *Now, Mr. Castillo, who has custody of your four children at this time?*

R: Angelina, su señoría.

(IJ looks straight at the camera.)

IJ: *I see. Why didn't you apply for asylum in the first place, Mr. Castillo?*

R: Necesito salir del penal para sacar a mis hijas del *Child Protective Services*. Me dijeron que tenía que comprar una casa para meter a las niñas.

IJ: *Let me read my notes, sir—*

(R begins talking, interrupting the IJ.)

R: Su señoría, su señoría, yo le ruego que me deje salir del penal para liberar a mis hijos del *CPS*, *in LA*. Yo necesito a mis hijos, su señoría. Ellos son lo que más quiero en esta vida, su señoría.

IJ: *Mr. Castillo, I am denying your applications for Asylum, Withholding and CAT, and I am ordering your removal to Mexico—Please, officer, give the respondent an appeal package.*

(ICE agent hands a package of documents to R.)

IJ: *I am giving you an application package and a deadline by which BIA must receive that package if you wish them to review your appeal.*

(R talks while looking at the interpreter.)

R: ¿Y quién cuida a mis hijas, señor?

(IJ pauses and looks away from the camera.)

IJ: *Now, sir, you'll have thirty days to present your appeal package to the Board of Immigration Appeals. Along with that package, I am giving you a fee waiver request form in case you cannot afford the fees for the appeal application.*

R: Gracias, su señoría, gracias. ¡Dios le bendiga!

IJ: *Now, you can ask ICE to allow you to apply for the U visa. For that you must file with them the I-246 application, the Application for a Stay of Deportation or Removal.*

R: ¿Me permitiría usted salir bajo fianza, su señoría?

IJ: *Okay, Mr. Castillo, let's talk about bond then. What's the position of the government on bond, Ms. Chang?*

ACC: *Your Honor, I am asking this court to deny bail because the respondent is a flight risk. Quite honestly the respondent's equities are near none. The respondent was served several bench warrants for criminal matters and never showed up in court. The respondent at the present moment doesn't have an address in the U.S. There is no evidence that the respondent has solid family ties in the U.S. At the moment there is no application for relief filed with this court. As a matter of fact, all applications have been denied. There is no history of employment and filing taxes. The respondent admitted himself that the sole reason he came to the U.S. was searching for the American dream.*

(There's a long silence, only interrupted by the ICE agent.)

ICE agent: *Judge, are you still there? I can't seem to hear anything from the screen.*

IJ: *We're here. I apologize. I was reviewing my previous notes. All right, please listen up and this is my decision. After reviewing your motion for bond, Mr. Castillo, I'll set bond at twenty thousand dollars. As you heard the assistant chief counsel, Ms. Chang, she alleged that you have failed several bench warrants, and for that reason the government thinks you could be a flight risk, so in order to guarantee you'll come to future hearings I'll set bond at twenty thousand dollars. If you are able to post bail, you'll be able* *to resolve all your matters out of the detention center. I wish you the best of luck. Case is adjourned.*

Tip!

Get acquainted with the criminal statute lingo of each state you travel in.

Well, quite honestly, whether you're traveling or not, it's important for you to get familiar with criminal law and statute lingo and its equivalent in Spanish. Remember that in some immigration court cases, what triggers a removal proceeding is that the respondent has one or more criminal convictions. For example, you will often hear ICE counsel requesting the respondent's "rap sheet" from the respondent's attorney (who may or may not have it in her file). A rap sheet contains convictions, charges, and dispositions that you will have to interpret or sight-translate. The information in rap sheets may come from municipal, county, district, state or supreme courts, as well as from federal courts, so the criminal component shouldn't be foreign to you. Master those criminal court terms.

Practice Lesson #2: Individual Hearings

Definitions:

> Evidentiary hearings on contested matters are referred to as individual calendar hearings or merits hearings. Contested matters include challenges to removability and applications for relief.[12]

> Hearings scheduled by the Immigration Court for testimony and evidence. These hearings are also known as "merits hearings."[13]

There are many types of individual hearings. They come in the form of an IJ's considering applications for cancellation of removal and for asylum, among other forms of relief.

Individual hearings take place in immigration courts and inside detention and transitional centers. In most cases, the immigration judge, an ICE assistant chief counsel, the respondent's attorney and the respondent will be present. A

---

[12] Immigration Court Practice Manual. 2018 Edition. Office of the Chief Immigration Judge. Naumchenko, Evgenia (Ed.). Independently published. 2019. Chapter 4 Hearings before the Immigration Judges. 4.16 Individual Calendar Hearing. (Retrieved on October 15, 2019)

[13] Immigration Court Practice Manual. 2018 Edition. Office of the Chief Immigration Judge. Naumchenko, Evgenia (Ed.). Independently published. 2019. Glossary. Individual Calendar Hearing. (Retrieved on October 15, 2019)

security guard and witnesses may be in the courtroom as well. Expert and forensic witnesses sometimes attend the sessions, although on many occasions they will testify telephonically.

Let's focus on one type of individual hearing: asylum hearings. These are the most difficult for interpreters. There are many reasons why: the length of the cases, the number of witnesses, the levels of complexity and the amount of terminology, slang and cultural components you have to know and deal with for a given case. They are also difficult due to the subject matter: testimony about traumatic events suffered by the respondent or fears he has of returning to his home country. In addition, when you interpret for asylum cases you must understand that each country is like a different world and even within one country you will often find different idiomatic phrases and slang, depending on the region.

Why is all this important? Simply because memorizing vocabulary for one country is not enough. The Hispanic world is vast. In spite of the fact that Spanish is the common language, individual usage is embedded in a diverse array of regionalisms, slang and influences from foreign languages. So, a good solution is to anticipate, prepare and take notes. Later in this book, we'll devote more time to strategies for preparing your game.

Consecutive interpreting in individual hearings—note-taking

After a long master calendar or a gruesome individual hearing, at around one in the afternoon Zoe is often exhausted and has probably forgotten everything said during the case—especially if it was one of those cases with lots of twists and turns, new words and slang. Or it may have been a complex case and her nerves got the best of her to the point that she could even forget the name of the person she interpreted for. Zoe thought that the exhaustion would only happen in her first few months of her interpreting career, but she came to realize she was exhausted because she was nervous. She got nervous because she thought that she was going to make a fool of herself, that she'd be embarrassed in front of everybody, that a respondent or someone from the gallery would say, "That's not the right word!" Before long, she decided to remedy that horrendous feeling and started taking good and copious notes. So if her memory failed her during a difficult hearing, she could rely on her notes. She'd been an excellent note-taker in college, and this new task wasn't that difficult.

Tip!

Always take notes. Bring plenty of notepads with you each time you interpret in immigration court. Also, do not forget your Spanish-English dictionary!

Note-taking has several advantages. During removal hearings, sometimes you'll encounter "evaluator-lawyers," who come to a hearing with a set of words memorized and try, via objections, to correct your choice of words in an unnecessary manner. Well, guess what—if you take notes, you'll have a record of what's being said, so you can clarify that you used synonyms. But only if you have your notes can you defend your interpretation. Hopefully, this fact will eventually discourage them from scrutinizing everything you interpret with a magnifying glass.

Another advantage of note-taking is that it helps you with word acquisition. Words used in context are easier to memorize. That's how you grow as an interpreter. Besides, those words and phrases will probably come back up over and over during the current or future cases. You also have a "written record" to study or peruse before your next time in immigration court.

Finally, taking notes provides you with some measured rhythm during your interpretation. It also helps you to stay focused and render even better interpretations because you're not relying only on your memory.

Remember to bring to individual hearings a glossary of the most important background information on each country of the Hispanic world. Create a cheat sheet. Below is an example of the content you can include on your own cheat sheet. Feel free to add any detailed information you cannot memorize or words you have difficulty pronouncing before the hearing.

Country: _____

    (1) Departments or states, cities, municipalities, cantons

    (2) Educational system

    (3) Ethnic groups

    (4) Religions

    (5) Political parties

    (6) Political party in power

    (7) President

(8) Cabinets

(9) Sectors of the economy

(10) Main trades

(11) Slang terms

(12) Police force and rank insignia

(13) Army and rank insignia

(14) Weaponry

As a new interpreter you'll probably need to consult this cheat sheet during each hearing. Then use it to keep logging important elements of the hearing, such as simple and proper names, new words, phrases, idioms, slang and dates. You can also use your cheat sheet to anticipate what's coming as the case unfolds. You'll need to be alert!

Remember, you are the last person to arrive at the hearing. Your information about the case is zero; sometimes you don't even know the name of the respondent. It's sort of like being invited to a party but none of your friends gave you the names of the host or any of the important guests, much less information about their jobs or amusing stories about their lives. You have a lot of catching up to do. So, use any resources at your disposal, including your cheat sheet.

Tip!

In addition to your cheat sheet, *take good notes*.

Take special note of the names of cities, towns, municipalities and other words that are difficult to pronounce. The new words you have to look up early in the hearing will keep popping up, and you don't want to stumble or have to ask for a second or third time how to pronounce them. By now you should own those words! They will keep coming up during direct and cross-examination, redirect, witness interrogation, closing arguments and in the IJ's decision. Also, often the IJ or the ACC will rely on your pronunciation for those difficult multisyllabic words. So you might as well have them ready next to you on a piece of paper for the middle and end of the hearing because guess what—you'll be tired, and those words will be waiting on that piece of paper to help you.

Put yourself in the position of the respondent. A big responsibility rests on your shoulders. If you don't understand what's been said, are you going to be able to interpret it? So, study, prepare and memorize important names. If you don't understand something, let the IJ know, and ask for repetition.

Televideo individual hearings—the importance of note-taking

As mentioned earlier, master calendars and individual hearings are sometimes conducted from a remote location using a remote system with a television screen in the courtroom or office where you're located. The remote system is also used for asylum cases where the respondent is detained. In such a case, everybody else is in the courtroom: the IJ, the ACC, the respondent's lawyer, the respondent's family and you.

Panic Point!

One afternoon, after Thiago had already interpreted at a morning master calendar, he went to a different courtroom for another hearing. Once in the interpreter's booth, he learned that this was an individual hearing by videoconferencing. Everybody was present in the courtroom except the respondent, whose face showed up on the TV screen.

From the first question asked by his attorney, the respondent couldn't stop talking and answering questions with long utterances and detailed narration. How do you prepare for this blast of information coming at you nonstop? What would you do?

This is a time when you need to have your note-taking skills ready.

Thiago wondered for the whole hearing whether this was a strategy of the respondent's attorney. The respondent was very emotional, even angry at times. He wanted to be heard and to win the case. His attorney didn't make any attempts to stop his client; after all, his client was speaking and it was up to Thiago to interpret and convey every detail of his story. It was also a critical and very sad case. Needless to say, Thiago wanted to make sure he was interpreting every word.

In situations like this, IJs usually stop the hearing and caution the respondent that in order to get the interpretation in the record, they need to speak slowly and loudly in short phrases and must pause when the interpreter requests it. But if this doesn't happen, you should ask the respondent to pause.

Tip!

Practice interpreting visualizing the respondent's story.

Shifts for individual hearings

Some individual hearing sessions start as early as 8 a.m. Other common start times are eight thirty, nine or nine thirty. You'll also have combo shifts for individual hearings such as eight and one, eight thirty and one, and nine and one. Also common are combos that start at eight thirty with the second at twelve thirty before breaking for lunch. You may also face combo shifts scheduled for eight and ten, with a break for lunch, then back at one and finally at three—all in one day, which is very demanding. Sometimes those shifts are for Asylum or Withholding of Removal, and Conventions Against Torture (CAT) cases or Cancellation of Removal cases.

On other occasions, you can spend a whole day on a single case, especially if there's a long list of witnesses testifying, including expert witnesses who may be testifying in person or telephonically.

In general, cases can take more or less time than anticipated, but the interpreter has to always be on the alert and assume that a hearing might take more than the scheduled time. Be aware of this when you are planning your schedule.

Why is this so important to know? Because that way you can plan your days, weeks and months way ahead. You may have other commitments—school, picking up kids from school or getting on a plane for a planned vacation—and you don't want to commit your time if you already have scheduled activities. Also include resting time based on your shifts. That way you don't burn out and fall prey to fatigue. Ask your coordinator for all the different shifts available to you before you commit.

Tip!

Organize and manage your workload.

Avoid booking several hearings on the same day or during a given shift. Never risk taking more than one case or planning any other activity. There shouldn't be any excuse on your part for being late or failing to attend a hearing.

Tip!

Always find a way to sleep and to rest!

Practice Lesson #3: An Inside Look at "The Hearing"

Why create a sample asylum hearing?

The answer is simple: There is no book written on the subject for the beginning interpreter, especially when considering complex individual hearings where the respondent is applying for Asylum, Withholding of Removal and the Convention Against Torture and Other Cruel, Inhuman or Degrading Treatment or Punishment (commonly known as the United Nations Convention Against Torture (UNCAT or CAT). Meanwhile, do you know how many mock trials and actual hearings IJs, respondent's attorneys and assistant chief counsels have been part of? *Countless*. Yet often a new interpreter comes to an asylum hearing without even having practiced once.

Tip!

Become familiar with forms and documents used in asylum cases.

The sample hearing relates only to the types of questions asked and preparation that lawyers do in Asylum, Withholding of Removal and CAT cases. This type of case is the longest and most difficult an interpreter and even attorneys and

IJs ever deal with in immigration court. The script only includes direct and cross-examination for you to practice.

In these types of hearings, the level of detail is at its maximum and is critical to the respondent's ability to make a strong case. Thus, interpreters have to travel deep into the nitty-gritty details of the countries in question. This asylum hearing will provide you with a chance to test your mettle in terms of requirements, stamina and commitment. This is so the new interpreter gets used to encountering words they've probably never heard before and to sample a wide variety of vocabulary, slang and terminology, all in one single case. Furthermore, this is a good opportunity for the new interpreter to become familiar with the language used in immigration courts, as it often differs from the language used in newspapers, journals, research papers or op-eds, which you can nonetheless study and use to prepare for these types of cases.

Unfortunately, there are a limited number of pages to achieve this goal, but "The Hearing" is still lengthy. It consists of direct examination by the respondent's lawyer and cross-examination by the ICE assistant chief counsel, as well as questioning by the IJ. Note that in immigration court hearings, unlike in other types of courts, the presiding official (here the IJ) can also question witnesses. He or she is not a silent entity sitting up on the bench.

In interpreting for asylum hearings, an interpreter speaks the language of people who have suffered persecution, torture and other forms of harm; asylum hearings also involve testimony of individuals who are victims of sex trafficking and extortion. At times, the testimony in these cases can be harsh, shocking and paralyzing—often unexpected for the new interpreter. With the sample hearing presented below, the goal is for you to see with your own eyes what kind of testimony occurs in these cases before you face your first real asylum case.

Horrendous or disturbing cases

During one of the first cases Juan Diego interpreted for—a cancellation-of-removal case—he froze up because he couldn't believe his ears. When he heard the assistant chief counsel talk to the IJ about the respondent, the words he used and his depiction of the crimes allegedly committed by the respondent were so heinous and horrendous he couldn't believe that person was actually sitting in front of him. Nevertheless, he had to process and then interpret those words into English. Juan Diego froze up and could not say a word.

It's hard enough to watch the TV news or read in newspapers stories about offenders molesting children or engaging in other inappropriate lascivious acts, let alone sit across from the accused perpetrator and have to process and say the words yourself. How do you prepare for that moment? Will you have a support system to help you deal with it? How do you deal with emotionally charged testimony during the hearing and afterward? What do you do before and after you interpret for these types of cases?

The vinegettes and sample hearing will give you a glimpse of what you'll have to hear and interpret in asylum cases, where you'll often hear about some of the goriest and dehumanizing acts that a person could suffer.

Anatomy of 'The Hearing': the respondent's attorney's direct examination, divided into blocks

Respondents' attorneys in removal proceedings *prepare* themselves and their clients before hearings. A competent attorney will review every document submitted in support of the asylum claim, including country conditions documentation,[14] other exhibits such as medical records and declarations from experts, and the asylum application itself (filed on Form I-589, often with a separate declaration). This should be done well before the day of the individual asylum hearing.

But perhaps it will make you feel better to know that the attorneys representing asylum applicants often divide their cases into blocks and that those blocks represent simple stories told from beginning to end. Sometimes the blocks follow a chronological order, sometimes not. Still, the stories move block by block.

This exercise gives you the opportunity to come up with your own interpretation for the questions in Spanish and the testimony in English, as these are not provided. Interpret these on your own and later consult your glossary and bilingual dictionaries to test yourself for accuracy.

While interpreting, record yourself. Let the recording be your evaluator.

---

[14] Immigration Trial Handbook. Maria Baldini-Potermin. § 7:17. Other claims for relief. Page 663. (Retrieved on October 5, 2019)

During your practice, try to interpret complete ideas while using the consecutive mode, which is usually how individual hearings are interpreted. Even when practicing with a classmate or a fellow interpreter, remember to take notes while you are using the consecutive mode. Also avoid memorizing slang and new words while practicing for the first time. Simply interpret what you can and *move on*. If you encounter slang or an unfamiliar word, use this technique: ask for clarification—you may need to consult the dictionary—and then *move on*. If slang or a new word hinders your interpretation, look it up and *move on*. What is it so important to practice interpreting from beginning to end? Because you will be simulating what happens in actual hearings and that will prepare you for your first few hearings. You have to be as ready as an experienced interpreter. Try to finish the entire material in one or two sessions. Then, you might want to review the material at a later time for the purpose of memorizing new words, phrases, slang and concepts.

At the end of Block 16, you'll see there is a recess: "Recess during direct examination (break for the interpreter)." There is also an implicit recess when the respondent's attorney ends his direct examination, which you'll see as "End of direct examination by Mr. Bollinger." After that, cross-examination starts by the assistant chief counsel, Ms. López. In an actual individual hearing, an IJ will often take a recess between direct and cross-examinations.

You'll notice throughout "The Hearing" that some words are in boldface. Bolded text refers to: Nahuatl words, Yaqui words, regionalisms from Sonora, narco-language or colloquialism from Mexico. You'll find their meaning in the alphabetic glossary in the back of the book. Use the glossary to review or consult while interpreting "The Hearing."

Remember!

Most of the slang in the hearing is unique to the state of Sonora and may not be applicable to other Mexican states.

If you cannot finish the interpretation in a single session, try doing "The Hearing" for a minimum of half an hour each time until your endurance increases.

If you are working alone, try recording all the parts and practice in increments of half an hour each time.

A note on sight translation: during actual immigration hearings, you'll very seldom be asked to sight-translate documents. It's usually done during master calendar hearings, applications for voluntary departure and cancellation-of-removal hearings.

Method to the madness:

Especially after interpreting for a couple of asylum cases, you will realize there is an organization to the "madness." Your brain will probably begin to recognize patterns, and those patterns turned into blocks of information. As you begin to ease into each block, you'll find that your brain starts getting comfortable in each block because it is easier to retrieve words. Your perception will be right! You'll find that discipline and the method to the madness in a document titled "Best Practices in Representing Asylum-Seekers."[15] It has been used as a guide to writing "The Hearing" and it should facilitate your brain's focus on a given family of words pertaining to a specific block or topic.

The fact that most respondent's attorneys prepare their cases and the hearing testimony by dividing the information into

---

[15] "Best Practices in Representing Asylum-Seekers." 2004. The American Law Institute. www.ali-aba.org/aliaba/RDVD01.asp (Retrieved on October 10, 2019).

blocks means that these hearings are not composed of random sets of questions. These blocks of information have some logic to them; they can be chronological or presented by topic, but they can be considered a story from beginning to end. It's the respondent's burden of proof to show that he or she is eligible for asylum. Attorneys for applicants always keep this in mind, but they also have to make it easier for their clients to remember what happened to make them fear returning to their country and to present that information in clear and easily understood testimony.

Also, a good attorney for an asylum applicant makes it easier for the client to transition his testimony from block to block. It's the attorney's responsibility to keep the client relaxed and focused, and that means helping the client to remember what must be proved to win asylum and to make smooth transitions in the testimony from topic to topic. This, fortunately, also gives the interpreter a chance to switch gears, breathe easy and then to zoom onto the next block of testimony.

The beginning questions in the asylum hearings are usually simple, designed to make the respondent/asylum applicant comfortable with the process, so they should be easier for you as well. But don't be fooled: one strange word or phrase could make you trip up and sweat *la gota gorda*—buckets. But for the most part, the first block is the easy section. There's no reason for you to get nervous or to make the respondent nervous. Use this section to warm up your vocal cords, adjust your volume and familiarize the respondent, witnesses and attorneys with the volume and tone of your voice and accent. If the hearing is conducted in the consecutive mode without the use of a headset, try to project your voice, making the sound loud and clear enough so that all those present understand you. Remember, the aim is always to make the testimony clear for the record. Keep in mind that this recording of your interpretation may travel through possible appeals.

Tip!

Anticipate! *Always be ready* for block-to-block transitions!

Even though the asylum applicant's lawyer is supposed to make transitions from block to block easy for his client, this sometimes doesn't happen. The attorney may choose to skip certain questions, may decide to change the order of the questions or may jump ahead in the chronology of the "story."

Or the IJ may ask the respondent's attorney to skip a block of questions because the IJ believes they are not relevant to the case or have already been answered. Thus, be alert and prepared for sudden changes of topic, and don't get too comfortable with a logical narrative or a particular sequence of events. That way, you're mentally prepared for anything that gets thrown at you.

Finally, you should be mindful that for "The Hearing," the blocks are packed with questions drawn from as many topics as possible, ranging from weapons and cars to drug trafficking and "narco style"—and even to music.

"The Hearing" is divided into twenty-three blocks that include direct examination by a fictional respondent's attorney, Mr. Bollinger, and eighteen blocks for cross-examination by a fictional assistant chief counsel, Ms. López.

If you read just the headings of the blocks listed below, they will give you a general overview of all the topics presented in "The Hearing" as well as the length of the exercise. That alone can be an exercise. As you read through the blocks, figure out possible questions that might arise from them; also come up with and jot down words, phrases and slang that you think you might encounter while interpreting for this case.

Direct examination by the respondent's attorney,

Mr. Bollinger:

BLOCK 1. Biographical information.

BLOCK 2. Schooling.

BLOCK 3. Abuse.

BLOCK 4. EMPLOYMENT

BLOCK 4.1. Employment: farmer.

BLOCK 4.2. Employment: builder.

BLOCK 4.3. Employment: narco-tunnels.

BLOCK 5. On account of membership in a particular social group—PSG 1 proposed: Mexican drug lord/kingpin/smuggler/trafficker who was given status of confidential informant and subsequent protection by Mexican authorities.

BLOCK 6. Threats. Altar Judicial Municipal Police.

BLOCK 7. Threats and attacks. The disappearance of the Chihuahua of García López's sister Guadalupe.

BLOCK 8. La Lupe's assassination. Shooting at Cerro Humo. Abduction and ransom.

BLOCK 9. Threat. Warning by Gaviota.

BLOCK 10. Sabotage against Naranjita, Mr. García López's pickup truck.

BLOCK 11. Narco-blankets. Mines; weapons; recruitment. Crime in the mine: El Águila kills Mota.

BLOCK 12. Narco-blankets job. Jesús, the target.

BLOCK 13. On account of membership in a particular social group—PSG 2 proposed:

Mexican drug lord/smuggler/trafficker who was given protection by a government entity, the local police and was working with cartels and instrumental in defying those cartels. Liaison.

BLOCK 14. Threats and sabotage perpetrated as result of informant job. Flashback: La Lupe's abduction. Rancho Los Güeros. Shooting weapons in the Cerro. Olive-green pickup truck on fire.

BLOCK 15. Anecdote, Rancho Elote: Kawis, Gaviota and Chavito.

BLOCK 16. Hospital General de Caborca. Threats: narco-blanket at the door.

[RECESS]

BLOCK 17. Incident at Rancho Elote with Gaviota and Chavito.

BLOCK 18. Protection house: Altar. Comandante Moreno. Transfer to Hermosillo protection house: La Mazmorra.

BLOCK 19. Federal shelter: Zócalo. Assault and escape.

BLOCK 20. Assault at Café La Rusa.

BLOCK 21. Assault at Zócalo.

BLOCK 22. Decision to leave Mexico. Entry to USA. Flashback: lookout.

BLOCK 23. Narco-style. Narco-corrido. Mariachis.

How the assistant chief counsel (ACC) conducts cross-examination

During cross-examination, the attorney for the government, the ICE assistant chief counsel, will have a series of questions, probably organized into blocks as well. The fundamental difference to keep in mind is that since the ICE attorney is in an adversarial position to the respondent who is seeking asylum, the questions will not necessarily come in chronological fashion and the questions are also not designed to guide or help the respondent in presenting his asylum claim. These questions are simply designed to test the respondent's credibility and the details of his claim. The ICE attorney's strategy is to show the weak spots in the respondent's testimony, to clarify confusing points in the respondent's story and, often, to confuse him. Their questioning often comes across as contemptible, harsh, testy, very dry and to the point.

So, what does this mean to you the interpreter? Brace yourself for sudden changes of direction, topic and tone. You may be tired by the time cross-examination comes along, so you must gather all your energies and focus. Don't think that because you're near the end you should sit back and relax. On the contrary, you may face new material not touched upon during direct examination, new topics and, hence, new words and confusing and contradictory questions and answers. Keep in mind also that ICE attorneys often do not have much (or any) questions prepared in advance of the hearing. Rather, they prepare their question list and/or topics as the respondent testifies.

Cross-examination by the assistant chief counsel,

Ms. López

BLOCK 1. Cross. Verify which authority apprehends Mr. García López.

BLOCK 2. Cross. Liaison between cartels and the police.

BLOCK 3. Cross. Narco-corrido.

BLOCK 4. Cross. Civilian vs. policeman. Police uniforms.

BLOCK 5. Cross. Security guard. Recruitment.

BLOCK 6. Cross. Beginnings as an informant.

BLOCK 7. Cross. ICE. Detention in Yuma, Arizona.

BLOCK 8. Cross. Sonora cartels. Narcos. Drug trafficking.

BLOCK 9. Cross. Lookout in the mountains. Security in the mines. Alias corroboration.

BLOCK 10. Cross. Nicknames. Revisiting jobs performed by García López for the cartels.

BLOCK 11. Cross. A tunnel to San Diego. Guitars or weapons?

BLOCK 12. Cross. Who is the alleged twin sister? Who is Mr. García? Fast and Furious operation. Weaponry.

BLOCK 13. Cross. Informant for the FBI, CIA or DEA? Segue to narcos, their pseudonyms: Who is who?

BLOCK 14. Cross. Narco-mansions exhibit, pictures.

BLOCK 15. Cross. Cartel collusion.

BLOCK 16. Cross. Trafficking methods.

BLOCK 17. Cross. Credibility. Mr. García López, a narco?

BLOCK 18. Cross. Last chapter: Zócalo.

This manual only provides you with direct and cross-examinations for "The Hearing." It's important for you to keep in mind that in actual asylum hearings you will have many more sessions to interpret. Following, you'll find a typical asylum hearing structure:[16]

- General instructions by the presiding IJ (usually in the simultaneous mode of interpretation).

- Preliminary matters pertaining to the case: marking of exhibits, any modification of the asylum application on Form I-589. Swearing as to the accuracy of the I-589 by the respondent and then signing the Form I-589 in front of the IJ.

---

[16] "Best Practices in Representing Asylum-Seekers." 2004. The American Law Institute. www.ali-aba.org/aliaba/RDVD01.asp (Retrieved on October 10, 2019)

- Advisals: (a) Pertaining to filing a frivolous application for asylum. (b) Change of address (usually in the simultaneous mode of interpretation).

- Opening statements by respondent's attorney and ICE assistant chief counsel. (simultaneous mode of interpretation).

- DIRECT EXAMINATION by the respondent's attorney (typically in the consecutive mode of interpretation).

- CROSS-EXAMINATION by the assistant chief counsel (typically in the consecutive mode of interpretation).

- Direct examination of an expert witness (such as a doctor, psychologist or psychiatrist), live or by phone (simultaneous mode of interpretation).

- Direct examination of a country-conditions expert (an expert with a PhD in cultural anthropology, for example, or a university professor), live or by phone (simultaneous mode of interpretation).

- Cross-examination of any expert witness (simultaneous mode of interpretation).

- Direct examination of any other witness for the respondent (consecutive mode of interpretation).

- Cross-examination of any other witness for the respondent (consecutive mode of interpretation).

- Presentation of any government witness, such as a documents forensic expert (simultaneous interpretation).

- Cross-examination of government's witness (simultaneous mode of interpretation).

- Closing argument for the respondent's attorney (simultaneous mode of interpretation).

- Closing argument by government attorney (simultaneous mode of interpretation).

- The immigration judge's oral decision (simultaneous mode of interpretation). Note, however, that an IJ may take case "under advisement" and not render an oral decision on the day of the hearing. Rather, the IJ's decision will come in written form and be mailed to the parties at a later date.

- Appeals rights advisals (simultaneous mode of interpretation).

Tip!

Anticipate! Anticipate! Anticipate!

When traveling, bring with you a good bilingual dictionary that includes slang and idiomatic phrases, and always keep abreast of the information pertaining to Latin American countries when it comes to human rights, politics and topics that come up during asylum hearings.

Tip!

When in doubt, use the appropriate technique to ask for clarification of words.

Here's an example: "Your Honor, may the interpreter clarify a matter regarding the use of the word foot in the source language?"[17]

---

[17] Nebraska State Courts Interpreter's Ethics Manual. Copyright © 2014. Nebraska Supreme Court/Administrative Office of the Courts

Note that you should always clarify in the third person. For example: "Your Honor, the interpreter needs clarification of the word *chanclas*."

Particular social groups for the respondent: what is in the mind of the respondent's attorney?

As noted earlier, it is the respondent's legal burden to prove eligibility for asylum and thus to prove either past persecution on account of race, religion, nationality, political opinion or membership in a particular social group.[18] An often difficult aspect of an asylum claim for a respondent is being able to establish membership in a particular social group (PSG). During some asylum hearings, you'll hear the IJ ask the respondent's attorney to state the particular social group in question unless it has been previously articulated. On other occasions, the attorneys and the IJ discuss the issue of the PSG off the record

---

https://supremecourt.nebraska.gov/sites/default/files/Program s/ethics-manual.pdf. (Retrieved on October 10, 2019)
[18] "A noncitizen seeking asylum must establish that the persecution that he suffered or that he fears is on account of race, religion, nationality, political opinion, or membership in a particular social group." As quoted in: Immigration Trial Handbook. Maria Baldini-Potermin. § 6:53 "On account of" element and five grounds of persecution. Page 441. (Retrieved on October 5, 2019)

before the hearing starts. Some IJs are meticulous and ask for this articulation beforehand, sometimes even during the master calendar hearing.

Also, during asylum hearings you'll hear the IJ ask the respondent's attorney to focus the direct examination on the PSG claimed.

For "The Hearing," you'll see examples of particular social groups that Mr. Bollinger could mention during the hearing; you might either write these down before the beginning of your practice session or keep this in mind throughout the hearing.

Disclaimer: The PSGs mentioned during "The Hearing" *do not* represent a legally accurate basis for the asylum claimed presented. They are fictional illustrations of the PSG concept presented for the sole purpose of language and interpretation practice. Note that they might not reflect the reality of an actual asylum case.

During actual asylum hearings, it might be useful to memorize the PSG. It might also be a good idea to write the PSG down on your memo pad to refer to later if needed.

Sometimes during direct examination, the IJ will remind the respondent's attorney to focus on the PSG—for example, if the IJ feels the attorney is taking too long or is deviating from the subject or is wasting time with questions not relevant to the claim and/or the PSG being claimed. If the PSG is fresh in your mind when it's mentioned during an actual hearing—sometimes more than once—you'll be ready to interpret it!

First particular social group proposed (PSG 1):

Mexican drug lord/kingpin/smuggler/trafficker who was given [the] status of confidential informant and subsequently protected by the Mexican authorities.

Second particular social group proposed (PSG 2):

Mexican drug lord/smuggler/trafficker who was given protection by a government entity, the local police and was working with cartels and instrumental in defying those cartels.

Proving points of fact:

The respondent's attorney must tackle establishing the following points of fact[19] in addition to establishing the PSG. These facts

---

[19] "Best Practices in Representing Asylum-Seekers." 2004. The American Law Institute. www.ali-aba.org/aliaba/RDVD01.asp (Retrieved on October 10, 2019)

are usually corroborated by documentary evidence in the form of exhibits. Next, you will see some of the facts that the respondent's attorney, Mr. Bollinger, has to establish in "The Hearing." You'll notice that the exhibits will start counting at Exhibit 7, and that is because there have been exhibits previously entered in the record and marked as evidence. These are documents that have nothing to do with proving the asylum claim. They usually include, for example, the NTA, the Form I-213, a change of address form, the notice of appearance as attorney (Form EOIR-28), etc.

Facts and their corresponding exhibits to be established by the respondent's attorney during "The Hearing":

Fact #1: R's identity:

> Exhibit #7: Birth certificate
>
> Exhibit #7A: Translation of birth certificate
>
> Exhibit #8: Mexican passport
>
> Exhibit #8A: Translation of Mexican passport

Fact #2: R grew up in Altar municipality and went to school in the Cerro Carneros

> Exhibit #9: R's picture with elders outside a church

Exhibit #10: R's picture around eight years old at the "Escuelita" in Cerro Carneros

Fact #3: R's family nexus:

Exhibit #11: Picture of R and his sister Guadalupe García

Fact #4: R lived in Sonora his adult life:

Exhibit #12: Picture of R in front of a ranch with a sign: "Altar Ranch"

Exhibit #13: Picture of R on the roof of a brick house with friends, the Altar church in the background

Exhibit #14: Picture of R inside an orange pickup truck with banners that read "Constructora Querobabi"

Exhibit #15: Picture of R inside an olive-green pickup truck with banners that read "Constructora Querobabi"

Fact #5: R lived in Hermosillo:

Exhibit #16: Picture of R on the roof of a brick house with a woman and a child. A street sign behind them reads: *"BIENVENIDOS A HERMOSILLO. Historia, cultura, y tradición 319 años"*

Exhibit #17: Picture of R in an Audi R8 Spyder sports car outside of the brick house

Fact #6: R in Otay Mesa, San Diego, United States; narco-tunnels:

>Exhibit #18: Picture of R in Otay Mesa, San Diego, United States, showing self-storage business "Time to Store" with R and two other unidentified men.

Fact #7: Attacks against R:

>Exhibit #19: Picture of a burned pickup truck with banner that reads "Constructora Querobabi"

>Exhibit #20: Picture of narco-blanket message at the entrance of R's ranch in Altar municipality

>Exhibit #20A: Translation of narco-blanket message

Fact #8: More threats:

>Exhibit #21: Picture of narco-blanket message with the name Jesús

>Exhibit #21A: Translation of narco-blanket message with the name Jesús

Fact #9: R as a liaison for the narco:

>Exhibit #22: Picture of a mariachi band at a party in Hermosillo with R and several known narcotraffickers

Fact #10: R's hospitalization due to narcos' attack.

Exhibit #23: R's discharge record from Hospital Caborca in Sonora, Mexico

Exhibit #23A: Translation of R's discharge record

Exhibit #24: Narco-blanket message in front of R's hacienda while R was at the Hospital General Caborca

Exhibit #24A: Translation of the narco-blanket

Fact #11: R lived in CDMX under the protection of the Mexican government:

Exhibit #25. Picture of R at the entrance of the federal shelter Zócalo with unnamed men

Exhibit #26: R's Mexican *cedula* (identification card) from CDMX

Exhibit #26A: Translation of R's identification card

Fact #12: R visits Café La Rusa in CDMX:

Exhibit #27: Receipt from Café La Rusa in CDMX with the phone number of a woman R was seeing

Exhibit #27A: Translation of receipt from Café La Rusa

Fact #13: R fled to USA, crossing from Altar to El Sásabe in Mexico into Arizona, United States:

Exhibit #28: R's selfie in the Altar Municipality

Exhibit #29: R's selfie in El Sásabe, Sonora, Mexico

Exhibit #30: R's selfie in the Buenos Aires National Wild Refuge

Fact #14: R's disappearance from Sonora, Mexico:

Exhibit #31: Newspaper article: Jesús García, notable business owner, disappears from Altar Municipality, his properties ransacked

Exhibit #31A: Translation of newspaper article: Jesús García, notable business owner, disappears from Altar Municipality, his properties ransacked

Fact #15: R's unwillingness to return to Mexico due to retaliation by cartels:

Exhibit A: Mexico country conditions, U.S. Department of State

Fact #16: R fears persecution[20] by cartels and the police if returned to Mexico:

---

[20] Immigration Trial Handbook. Maria Baldini-Potermin. § 6:52 Definition of persecution. Page 438. (Retrieved on July 6, 2020)

Exhibit B: "Mexico: Organized Crime and Drug

Trafficking Organizations," Congressional Research

Service[21]

Fact #17: R was unable to protect himself from cartel retaliation:

Exhibit C: Report on Mexican police corruption.

"Mexico's Police. Many Reforms, Little Progress," by

Maureen Meyer[22]

Nonverbal responses

Included in the "The Hearing" are nonverbal responses. Below

are some examples:

(R points at his chest and remains silent.)

(R nods.)

(R raises his hand.)

(R points at his nape.)

(IJ interrupts D.)

---

[21] "Mexico: Organized Crime and Drug Trafficking
Organizations." Congressional Research Service.
https://fas.org/sgp/crs/row/R41576.pdf (Retrieved on
December 20, 2019)
[22] Meyer, Maureen. "Mexico's Police. Many Reforms, Little
Progress." Washington Office on Latin America, 2014.
https://www.wola.org/sites/default/files/Mexicos%20Police.pd
f (Retrieved on November 19, 2019)

The use of nonverbal responses is a common occurrence during removal hearings. You'll experience both short and extensive nonverbal responses given by respondents. When that happens, you might remain silent because, officially, gestures don't need to be interpreted. Now what if the IJ looks at you, the interpreter, expecting to provide an answer? What would you do then? In such cases, you may simply say, "Your Honor, the respondent gestured and no utterances accompanied it." The IJ may then repeat the question and instruct the respondent to provide a verbal answer.

More nonverbal responses:

(R cries.)

(R sobs.)

(R laughs.)

(R sneezes.)

Needless to say, you are not supposed to imitate any of the above sounds. Nonetheless, you'll hear the IJ put on the record some of the noises made by the respondent, especially if they are in direct response to a given question. This is especially true if the respondent is crying or sobbing.

(Pauses)

Pauses are also included in "The Hearing," appearing as "(pause)." Pauses are self-explanatory: they are used when someone pauses during the hearing, either because the person deems it necessary to pause or because the interpreter or IJ requests it. Sometimes there's an objection from one of the lawyers or there's a long pause either because the respondent is thinking about an answer or because a lawyer is reformulating a question.

Curse words

Just one word for the interpreter on this topic: VERBATIM.

How to deal with interruptions

In "The Hearing," you will not see the numerous interruptions that happen during actual removal hearings. For example, your interpretation will probably be interrupted multiple times either by counsel coming up with new questions on the fly, by the IJ or even by the respondent answering questions without waiting for you to provide interpretation. You will only see a few interruptions during "The Hearing." It also often happens that in the heat of a hearing, the parties completely forget there's an interpreter and repeatedly speak on top of each other without letting you interpret. This disruption also occurs when the respondent understands and speaks English and anticipates the interpretation.

Some interruptions included in "The Hearing" are the phrases: *strike that!"* used when a lawyer doesn't want a question or the wording of a question to be part of the record; and *"objection!"* used when a lawyer opposes a testimony or evidence.

Strategies to use during individual hearings and during asylum cases in particular

For the reasons outlined above, you can often be at a disadvantage when you step into these types of cases as an interpreter. Thus, and because you should avoid surprises, you'll want to always try to minimize the number of potential problematic issues. If the agency that sends you for an assignment provides you with the respondent's country of origin for the case beforehand, brush up on information and articles about that particular country, especially on issues pertaining to domestic violence, gangs, religion and politics. IJs read reports about those countries to prepare for their cases all the time. At the very least, read the information in the cheat sheet that you created for that country before the hearing begins.

While in court waiting for your hearing, look around. Sometimes you'll find useful information about the case right in front of you. Look for scarves, strange clothes or T-shirts with slogans in the respondent's native language. Look at the respondent's table. How big is the file sitting on it? How many lawyers are representing her? These are like the clues to a puzzle and they may help you to close the circle.

Next, listen and take note of the evidentiary package. Does the case have lots of exhibits? What are they about? Take note! Are the documents all translated? Make a note of that, at least mentally. Did they say a word you're not familiar with? Look it up! Anticipate! Look for clues. Your case starts even before direct examination. Listen to any proper names or place names mentioned while the IJ is making them part of the evidence. These are all important because questions might arise from those names and information, and even if they don't you will probably have to correctly use and say those names in your interpretation.

Finally, don't get comfortable until it's all over and you are done with interpreting for the hearing. You should strive for perfection even though in reality it's almost impossible to attain, especially when you are interpreting your first hearings. If you develop good habits—you are prepared, rested and focused—you'll have a satisfactory interpreting session, maybe even a flawless one.

Tip!

Interpreter! The *evidence* is in front of you.

Do you see slim files or thick folders and packages of evidence or even boxes?

Do you see one attorney for the respondent or several lawyers at the desk?

Do you see the gallery full of family members and friends or just the respondent?

Do you see any props such as easels, diagrams or projectors? Yes? Well then, brace yourself for a long and complex hearing.

Pay attention to any exhibits mentioned or entered into evidence. Take note of that on a piece of paper because they offer you clues about the hearing. Did you hear *expert witness* or *forensic expert* mentioned? What about a witness list? Is it just the respondent or the spouse, children or in-laws? Members of the respondent's church? If there is an expert witness on board due to psychological issues present in the life of the respondent, chances are you'll be using simultaneous interpreting of the expert witness testimony.

Disclaimer: The characters and narratives used in this book are all fictional, created for teaching purposes only.

Practice Lesson #4: "The Hearing"

Exercise: interpreting for an asylum hearing

Instructions: Read the entire hearing below so you can become familiar with the way the text is laid out and be prepared to record yourself. Do not memorize it. Then record all parts: IJ, D, R, ACC, bailiff.

Interpret in the consecutive mode. Simultaneous mode should be used when attorneys object, refer to exhibits and speak to one another.

Settings:

(A) This hearing takes place in an immigration courtroom in the United States. You, the interpreter, are sitting to the left of the IJ, who can hear your voice without the microphone. The ACC's desk is located below and toward the right side of the IJ's bench, diagonally and approximately twenty feet from the interpreter's desk. Standing toward your left in front of you is a bilingual bailiff; she can hear your voice directly and you can hear her as well. The respondent's attorney's desk is located below and toward the left side of the IJ's bench, directly in front of you at ten feet from the interpreter's desk. The respondent is sitting in the witness stand, located to the right of the IJ's bench and approximately twenty-five feet from you; the witness stand has a microphone. You have to turn your head to see the respondent. In the gallery there are three bilingual paralegals and two additional attorneys at the respondent's desk.

(B) The respondent appears remotely; you'll see his face and hear his voice through the videoconferencing unit and a large TV screen. The other conditions remain the same.

Suggestions: Avoid memorizing the content for at least the first few practices of "The Hearing." If you run into a slang term, name or phrase you find impossible to interpret, use the appropriate technique to ask for clarification, look at your glossary and move on. Focus on interpreting with a steady flow. Try to go through the entire practice hearing at once, making believe you're in an actual hearing when you don't have much control in terms of pauses, interruptions, breaks and recess. Once you've interpreted all the material, go back and study slang, colloquialisms, names of weapons, narco-related terms and so on, and read the articles referenced throughout the hearing to deepen your knowledge of issues raised during the hearing. All this studying will help you to be better prepared for your job.

Attention: Slang terms are marked in **bold** throughout the exercise. Words and phrases in uppercase indicate that they are spoken louder and faster than normal speech. To facilitate the reading of the script, which is lengthy, I've used italics as a convention for participants speaking in English and non-italics for participants speaking in Spanish.

Commencement of hearing by the respondent's attorney, Mr. Bollinger, with direct examination

From the rear-left corner of the courtroom, a clerk comes out and loudly and clearly addresses the attendees.

Clerk: *All rise. The Honorable John Smith presiding in immigration court.*

After some preliminary matters are dealt with, the IJ instructs the respondent's attorney to begin direct examination.

BLOCK 1. Biographical information

D: *Sir, state your name for the record.*

R: GARCÍA **DE NACENCIA**.

(IJ takes his glasses off and stares at R.)

IJ: *Sir, provide your full and complete name for the record and please lower your voice.*

R: ¡HABLO FUERTE PARA QUE SE ME ENTIENDA, ES MI COSTUMBRE SEÑOR!

IJ: *Sir, step away from the microphone. Your name, please!*

R: Me inscribieron con apellidos García López y de nombres Jesús y Antonio.

D: *That is corroborated in evidence, Your Honor, under Exhibit numbers 7 and 7A, birth certificate and its translation, Tabs F and G, respectively.*

IJ: *Sir, have you used any other names, pseudonyms, monikers or aliases?*

R: ¿Alias? El Güero. El Güero, **de nacencia**. Así me llaman. Así es, El Güero. Más bien El Güero García, me llaman mis **noraguas** y mis **cuates**.

IJ: *Sir, did you have somebody helping you to fill out your application for asylum, form I-589?*

R: Este, este, sí, la señorita Yooko Quintanilla del bufete de mi asesor jurídico. El señor *Bollinger* me ayudó también, pero la historia que le conté, esa es mi historia, quiero que sepan. ¡Qué quede bien claro!

D: *Where were you born, Mr. García López?*

R: Estoy registrado en la villa Santa Gertrudis de Altar, municipalidad Altar, estado de Sonora, en los Estados Unidos Mexicanos.

D: *What's your date of birth, Mr. García López?*

R: El Día de los Santos Inocentes. El día que nadie debe creer a nadie. El veintiocho de diciembre de mil novecientos ochenta y ocho.

IJ: *Sir, are any of your kin coming to testify in court today?*

R: Nel, magistrado.

(D is looking down at the desk and shuffling through documents.)

D: *Are you married, Mr. García?*

R: Tengo **jaina**, una novia bien bonita, licenciado. Comprometidos estamos, eso sí. No quiero quedarme **cotorro**.

(IJ stands up, moves to a nearby copy machine and stares at R.)

IJ: *ARE YOU LEGALLY MARRIED, SIR?*

R: Estuve ajuntado con la señorita Bachia Banderas. Tuvimos un hijo, un **vuqui** que le puse Maaso, muy intranquilo el **churi**. Está hecho todo un **bato**.

D: *Jesús, where are your children?*

R: En los cerros… en el desierto… uno vive con su **ae**, *his mom*… el otro con su **asu**, *her granny*.

D: *Do you see them? Strike that!*

(R doesn't respond.)

D: *Do you talk to them?*

R: Pos, mire que no.

D: *Why not?*

R: ¡Ah! No se puede… te intersectan y ¿quién sabe si desaparecen a los **chavitos**? No vale la pena arriesgarlos, señor.

D: *Mr. García. have you been legally married to any of your girlfriends ever, here or in Mexico?*

R: Por la iglesia tratamos, pero nunca se dio.

D: *So, you're not legally married to any person in Mexico nor in the United States, Mr. García López?*

R: Muy posible es que me case con Mary Lourdes Carney, licenciado; pero la falta de **tomi** nos impide consumar matrimonio, usted sabe.

D: *ARE YOU MARRIED TO MS. CARNEY, MR. GARCÍA?*

R: Nel, licenciado, aún no, señor. Es mi **flance**, mi prometida.

IJ: *Did you ever get a Mexican passport, sir?*

(D interrupts IJ.)

D: *Your Honor, my client's translation of his Mexican passport appears in Exhibit 8A, Tab I, on page 21.*

IJ: *Can I see it? Can I see the original as well? Thank you, Counselor, and let's move on please.*

(The bailiff takes the passport from D's hands and walks over the bench to hand it to IJ.)

BLOCK 2. Schooling

D: *What's your highest level of schooling, Mr. García López?*

R: Escapé del tercer grado.

D: *So I assume you didn't finish the third grade. So why and where did you escape from, Mr. García López? Could you tell the court how and under what circumstances you escaped?*

R: Escapé porque fui maltratado. Me castigaron mucho, licenciado, recibí mucho golpe, muchos reglasos, **jodazos** y cachetadas que me dieron, licenciado. En la escuelita me castigaron como a un asno en el cerro. Tengo de testigo a los tantos **churis** que vieron tanto abuso.

IJ: *YOU DON'T HAVE AFFIDAVITS FROM THOSE CLASSMATES, DO YOU, SIR?*

R: **Ahorita** no, magistrado, ¿quién sabe qué se hizo del **criaturero**?

D: *And where did you go to school?*

R: En las alturas de Cerro Carnero.

D: *And where is that located?*

R: A pocos kilómetros del municipio Altar.

D: *And every morning you walked to the school, Mr. García? Isn't that true?*

R: Pos sí, no había helicóptero.

(IJ cackles and turns and looks at the interpreter, smiling.)

D: *Jesús, were you scared to go to school?*

R: ¡Aterrado, señor! Sudaba solo pensar tener que subir los cerros.

D: *Jesús, I am going to call your attention to what is being marked as Exhibit 10 that's on Tab K, on page 23.*

(The bailiff hands the exhibit to R.)

D: *Do you see yourself in that picture?*

R: *Yes!*

D: *Can you tell this court who is in that picture?*

R: Jesús Antonio García López, señores.

D: *Where was that picture taken?*

R: El cerro queda detrás… la escuelita está a un lado… es Cerro Carneros, licenciado.

D: *Who took that picture, Jesús?*

R: El maestro.

BLOCK 3. Abuse

D: *Sir, you mentioned you were terrified. Those were the words you just used—why?*

R: Por la **castigada**, la penitencia, licenciado.

D: *Who punished you, Mr. García López? I mean, who was the perpetrator of the abuse or abuses against you?*

R: Eulogio Petulio, licenciado. Él pasaba por los puestos y ¡**riata!** me daba un **jodazo** en la mera **tatema**. Me tenía intimidado. Era **de insultada a insultada**. Me sonaba duro, a diestra y siniestra, entonces los **vuquis** se burlaban de mí. El hijo de la gran puta me castigó duro, me forzó a hacer cuclillas con librotes pesados en los hombros o en la cabeza y cuando no lo hice me, me, me golpeó duro. Me golpeó con una regla de madera pesada, a veces enfrente de la **vucada**, por eso escapé del tercero, señor.

D: *Who is Eulogio Petulio, Mr. García López?*

R: Un ambulante… Había maestros que iban y venían al pueblito por meses, después se marchaban. El señor Petulio era un improvisado y fue responsable porque odiara la escuelita y las clases.

D: *Did Mr. Petulio abuse you sexually, Mr. García López?*

R: Nunca lo permití, licenciado… Petulio trató.

D: *Did Petulio take the picture I showed you moments ago?*

R: Pos sí.

(R pauses and stares at IJ.)

R: Más de una vez.

D: *And you escaped—and what did you do after you left the school,*
Mr. García López?

R: Chambear, chambear duro, licenciado.

BLOCK 4.1. Employment: farmer

D: *What kind of jobs did you do, Mr. García López?*

R: Tendría unos diez años de edad y me fui a **chambear** a los campos… fue cuando sembré por vez primera marihuana, allá por Bacadéhuachi, por Nácori y en Sarahuipa, estado de Sonora.

D: *You were ten or eleven years old—you were a kid. Who took you to work in the marijuana fields or did you go by yourself, Mr. García?*

(R sneezes.)

R: *Sorry, sorry, I am sorry.* Me llevó un primo mayor, con él me escapé a los sembrados, señor licenciado.

D: *What is the name of that cousin and how old was your cousin at the time, Mr. García López?*

R: En el caserío le llamaban **Maaso**, que en lengua **yaqui** quiere decir "Venado Cola Blanca". Él era mayor que yo, tendría veintiún años, por ahí. **Maaso** corría y bailaba como un venado, era un **chavo** simpático, nos parecíamos mucho, era como un hermano mayor. Tanto él como yo sufrimos del abuso. Compartíamos el mismo dolor. Él no quiso ir a la escuela nunca más. Fue él quien me dijo que la **tekia**, el oficio, lo curaba todo, esas fueron sus palabras y me fui de aventuras con el **Maaso**.

IJ: *MOVE ON, COUNSELOR!*

D: *So, you grew cannabis, and then what did you do next, Mr. García López?*

R: Maaso desapareció… unos dicen que lo metieron preso por **burrero** de una banda local de narcos… otros decían que era sicario de los Zetas, la verdad es que la tierra se lo tragó.

D: *Then what did you do? Did you go back to your town in Cerro Carnero, Mr. García?*

R: Este, este, este… sí, sí… **recalé** al cerro Carnero y un padrastro **gomero**, el padre de mis medias hermanas Alma y Bernarda me llevó a las sierras, al cultivo de la amapola.

D: *What was your line of work?*

R: Mi primera **chamba** consistió en sacarle el jugo pegajoso a la flor… es **chamba** solo para chavos… Sembré la flor de amapola también, pero terminé haciendo labores de deshierbe, de secado y de empaque del producto final… **Y luego luego** de la redada de "Los chavos del opio", nunca más me permitieron regresar al opio.[23]

D: *Where did you work in the opium poppy business, Mr. García López?*

R: En las sierras de Altar, en el Valle del Yaqui, era por todo el estado de Sonora, licenciado.

D: *Who did you refer to as "Los Chavos del Opio," Mr. García?*

R: Los niños que allí le hacen a la **chamba** del opio; son los **vuquis**. Ellos son los que rallan la amapola que encuentran en los surcos, **a ráis** y bajo el sol, caminan los surcos, señor licenciado.

D: *How old were you when you worked in the poppy fields, Mr. García?*

R: Unos quince años, pero parecía tusa de maíz, parecía que tenía cinco o seis. Estaba **güilo**, licenciado.

D: *Did you do any other work as a farmer, Mr. García López?*

---

[23] Pigeonutt, V. (13 de julio, 2015). Los niños del opio en Guerrero. *El Universal*. Recuperado de http://www.eluniversal.com.mx/articulo/estados/2015/07/13/los-ninos-del-opio-en-guerrero#imagen-1

R: Sembré y recogí milpas, avena, alfalfa y pasto para forraje. Cultivé el sorgo en Coahuila…

(R pauses, scratches his head and stares at D, appearing to consider whether to continue or not. In a split second, D gestures to R to proceed with testimony.)

R: Pos… luego luego… cultivé flores de ornato en Querétaro, como la flor de noche buena y el campasúcil. Hmmmm… coseché milpas en Jalisco, fui trabajador migrante en mi propio país, licenciado. Mi padre me dijo que era buen campesino y que un día iba a **chambear** al norte, **al otro lado.**

IJ: *How old were you at that time, Mr. García?*

R: Tendría unos dieciocho o diecinueve años, señor. **¡Añil!**

IJ: *Your witness, Mr. Bollinger.*

BLOCK 4.2. Employment: builder

D: *So, Jesús, Petulio's actions made you leave school and you're forced to work in the fields. Did you work in any other industry or employment as a youth?*

R: Constructor soy, licenciado. Le hice a la construcción desde **bato**. Le eché con ganas al cemento, arena y ladrillos, señores licenciados.

D: *What kind of construction jobs did you perform, Mr. García López?*

R: Albañilería, licenciado. Yo puse bloques, ladrillos, construí muros de cantos de piedras, eché mezcla de cemento y arena. Hice mucha albañilería. Abrí muchos huecos también, licenciados. **¡Añil!** Claro que sí, licenciado.

D: *Is there any project or job that brings any memories to you, Mr. García López?*

R: **¡Añil!** Le hice a la construcción de narco-mausoleos y de las narco-colonias, grandototas hechas para buchones. **Luego luego, chambeé** lo de los túneles y hasta en una que otra pista clandestina de aterrizaje en medio de los cerros.[24]

D: *How did you get that kind of employment in the construction arena, Mr. García?*

R: Con un cuñado, el señor Refugio Dorame.

D: *Why would they employ you on a regular basis, Mr. García López?*

R: Era joven y ya tenía fama de echarle el cuerpo a la **chamba**, donde se suda duro. Era muy listo además, no era ni vago ni **retobado**, de lo que algunos me acusaron.

---

[24] Sánchez, D. (7 de abril, 2019). Policía Federal destruye pista de aviación clandestina en Sonora. *Excelsior*. Recuperado de https://www.excelsior.com.mx/nacional/2017/08/15/1181868

D: *Who taught you the trade in masonry, Mr. García López?*

R: El pariente, el cuñado, el señor Dorame.

(R pauses. IJ interrupts R's silence and turns to the interpreter.)

IJ: *Interpreter, could you spell all the names for the record, please?*

D: *So, where for the first time did you get your hands dirty in the field of construction and for whom did you start working, Mr. García López?*

R: Fue en Querobabi donde aprendí a fabricar ladrillos a mano, licenciado. Estaba yo bajo la tutela del señor Refugio Dorame. Fue él quien me llevó a construir bodegas a los pueblos aledaños; por allá puse lozas en patios, levanté mausoleos para narcos. El señor Dorame manejaba su viejo **charangón**, de villa en villa. Él me daba de comer… Sepa usted, donde hubo **chamba** hubo comida y techo, allí en las mismas obras se dormía bien, licenciado.

D: *Did you then continue working with your brother-in-law, Mr. García López?*

R: **Nel**, licenciado, el tío Piedra me llevó con él a otras muchas obras.

D: *Okay, Okay, Mr. García, now I want you to share with the court what it was like working with your relative. Did you perform any other jobs for him?*

R: A poco me usaban para llevar y traer agua, alimentos y recaditos, pero cuando me rezagaba con el agua, las **coyotas** y el café, me zurraban y me ponían a abrir fosas. "Agarra el pico y pala Zorrito", me decían. Ya durante el almuerzo, era yo dando pico y pala. Era esqueleto yo, parecía un **chapayeka**, y después me dejaban tranquilo para que me comiera las **horruras**, las sobras de sus burros, sus **machihui** y unos **dogos**, señor, pero no mucho quedaba. **¡Mmmta!** Tuve que **ruñir** cáscara de cuanto fruto le tiraron al chancho, licenciado. Así no se podía vivir por mucho tiempo, en tanto en el campo tenía comida segura; allá se robaba gallinas. Aprendí a cazar con una **resortera** y si no hallaba en la caza, comía las milpas crudas. Tenía estómago de hierro, duro, muy duro, licenciado, muy duro.

BLOCK 4.3. Employment: narco-tunnels

D: *Mr. García López, you indicated in your written affidavit attached to your application I-589 that you've worked in the tunnels. Could you explain to us what type of tunnels you are referring to and for how long you did that line of work?*

R: Ah qué sé yo, licenciados… fueron cientos de hoyos… Me llevaron a la faena con los tíos López y Frías… por entonces ya sabía fabricar ladrillos y tejas con mis propias manos, abría fosos también, cisternas, y albercas. **Ahorita** recuerdo que me fui al primer túnel con un **chavo** yóreme que compraba cabras en el rancho, me dijo que había mucha **lana** y **morras**, me convenció **el chavo**. Primero fuimos a unas naves a cargar sacos de harina y trigo, muy cerca de puerto Guaymas, por allá debajo de las montañas en el mismo desierto Altar, casi frontera con *Arizona*. Allí trabajé en el primer hoyo… **Luego luego**, mi **camarada** apareció en una cuneta enterrado, sobre una loma de polvo blanco. La gente creyó que era harina, **pos** había sacos abiertos alrededor, pero era *fentanyl*. Yo nunca vi un centavo de lo que **chambeé** en aquel hoyo, entonces me fui de ayudante de albañiles, a cargar arena… cargué cemento también, cargué costales de tierra, pero no pude aguantar el hambre… parecía yo una espiga de sorgo, licenciado. Entonces, me regresé a Cerro Carneros y en el pueblo trabajé para mis tíos Rafael y Mario. Mis tíos, **luego luego**, me llevaron a la **chamba** de los túneles.

D: *Aha! So, how did your uncles López and Frías end up taking you to work with them, Mr. García López?*

R: Ellos tenían la **chamba**, y necesitaban ayudante… Recuerdo que por aquel tiempo, vivía yo con el tío Piedra, pero los otros eran más fuertes y avispados y ganaron apuesta para llevarme **a chambear** con ellos.

D: *Would escaping have been an option, Mr. García López?*

R: Eran hombres mayores y fuertes y me encontrarían donde quiera que me metiera, licenciado. Les tenía mucho miedo y sobre todo tenía miedo estar solo, a decir verdad, siempre anduve acompañado, alguien siempre me cuidó; podría caer yo, en manos de un **pollero** o sicario o terminar de esclavo para pandillas, licenciado.

D: *You mentioned a bet?*

R: Pos sí, lanzaban un **tecolín** al aire y el que ganaba, ganaba el derecho de mis manos.

D: *Got it! So then what did you do next, Mr. García López?*

R: En las obras cargué agua para los **topos**,[25] son los esclavos, a los que obligan abrir hoyos, y cargar piedras. Los capataces se hacen pasar por **polleros**, los engañan diciéndoles que los van a pasar **al otro lado** y terminan convirtiéndolos en esclavitos, a los

---

[25] Sánchez, L. (24 de marzo, 2013). Topos: los esclavos del narco. *El Universal.* Recuperado de https://archivo.eluniversal.com.mx/estados/89921.html.

pobres soñadores, licenciado. Una vez que quedan atrapados, no los dejan ver la luz del sol. ¡A dar pico y pala, licenciado!

D: *You just mentioned and defined the word* topos *as slaves of the tunnels. Were you a "topo," Mr. García López?*

R: No, yo fui un obrero, gracias a mis tíos.

D: *Mr. García López, did you possess any skills that made you suitable for that type of work? Why did you stick to building tunnels?*

R: **¡Añil!** Así es, licenciado. Yo podía meterme donde un hombrón no cabía; aunque hay agentes de patrulla fronteriza que se meten en los túneles, a esos les llaman ratas de túneles".[26]

D: *Do you know who was behind the construction of those tunnels you worked on, Mr. García López?*

R: Trabajé si no mal recuerdo… trabajé para los del Sinaloa, los del Pacífico y Jalisco Nueva Generación. Fueron muchos para los que trabajé, licenciado.

D: *And to clarify, those names you mentioned refer to government or private entities?*

---

[26] Wilkens, John. "Border Patrol's 'tunnel rats' stalk drug smugglers in an underground game of hide-and-seek." Los Angeles Times. November 26, 2017. https://www.latimes.com/local/lanow/la-me-ln-sd-tunnel-rats-20171126-story.htm. (Retrieved on May 15, 2020)

R: *Cartels, Mr. Bollinger.*

D: *Drug cartels!*

R: Añil, licenciado. Poder, fuerza y mucha **lana** construye hoyos y mucha, pero mucha mercadería pasa por los túneles, señores.

D: *How was it that you got ahead in the job as a tunnel worker, Mr. García López?*

R: Bueno, los capataces me preguntaron, "¿cómo le sabes tanto a la **chamba chavito**?", yo les decía que aprendía rápido, que tenía muchos oficios, entonces se reían de mí y me ponían a dar pico y pala y a escarbar por una o dos semanas y cuando comprobaban que yo, de veras, hacía muchos oficios, **pos** me ponían de patrón de **topos**, de los esclavos, aquellos que no pueden salirse del hueco, como les platiqué. No me gustaba mandar, pero sí me gustaba la **lana** que pagaban.

D: *Did you possess any other skills or were you knowledgeable of a trade that made you suitable for that kind of work, Mr. García?*

R: Bastante, licenciado.

D: *What skills did you possess, Mr. García?*

R: Sabía mucho, licenciado. Después de cavar hoyos las dos primeras semanas, me las pasaba dando opiniones para mejorar uno que otro trabajo, fuera de albañilería, electricidad o plomería; ya para el siguiente lunes… **pos** me subían a patrón de **topos**, como les dije.

D: *Did you get paid for doing that type of job, Mr. García López?*

R: Recibí de unos mil a mil trescientos y a veces mil quinientos pesitos, cada tres semanas. Me pagaban como maestro albañil, licenciado.

D: *Señor García López, por favor—if you know, what ever happened to Mr. Piedra?*

R: Nunca más lo vi… Para entonces ya no era yo albañil de media cuchara…Tampoco necesité su ayuda nunca más… pero el tío Piedra apareció en un potrero… apareció **encobijado**… así escuché en **un mentidero**.

D: *Was that a sign of anything, if you know, Mr. García?*

R: **Pos sí**, mire usted, o el señor estaba involucrado en las drogas o se negó a trabajar para los narcos, licenciados.

D: *Was your life in danger while working in the tunnels, Mr. García?*

R: Era un **chavo** yo, y mi vida peligraba en todas partes. Ahora, en la **chamba** de los túneles… los albañiles desaparecían cuando menos lo esperabas, pienso que los cárteles no querían arriesgarse con la información que teníamos. **Luego luego** me enteré de que era mejor para los capataces, desaparecer a los obreros que pagarles la plata, no era mera **feria** no, era muy

buena **lana**. Los capataces eran mezquinos, eran **codosduros**,

porque se dio casos donde albañiles y obreros iban a la

procuraduría a delatar a los capataces, porque no les pagaban…

Luego luego los desaparecían y cuando encontraban sus

cuerpos, aparecían en cunetas, tirados, abandonados sus cuerpos

aparecían… Tiene uno que andar con mucho cuidado,

licenciados.

D: *Did you enjoy giving orders? Did you think you could become a powerful*
leader?

R: **¡A poco!** No, no, no me gustó mandar, pero me gusta la

lana, licenciado.

D: *How were the working conditions inside the tunnels, Mr. García?*

R: Para mí bien… yo salía a respirar aire puro… ¿pero para los

topos? No les dejaban **resollar**. Yo hasta me daba el lujo de

dormir en pequeños cuartos que servían de almacén.

D: *How was it possible to stay employed and work from tunnel to tunnel,*
Mr. García?

R: Hacía mi trabajo, y no me metía a chismosear, ni metía mi

hocico donde no me incumbiese.

D: *Could you work in any of the trades you learned if you were to return to Mexico, Mr. García López?*

R: ¡Nel! A mí me matan antes de agarrar una **rajuela** de albañil, licenciado.

D: *Could you tell us, ballpark, in how many tunnels did you work?*

R: Cientos de pasadizos y laberintos, licenciados... Se cansa uno de estar allá abajo.

D: *Did you ever reach the United States through a tunnel?*

R: Esto, esto, esto... sí, la primera vez aparecí en Otay Mesa en San Diego y después un montón de veces más llegué a ese bello lugar.

D: *Mr. García López, I'd like to show you what's being marked as Exhibit 18, Tab Q, on page 31, a picture of Otay Mesa, in San Diego, showing a self-storage business with the name "Time to Store" and a group of men.*

(The bailiff hands a picture to R.)

D: *Mr. García López, do you recognize that picture?*

R: *Yes, I do!* El del sombrero negro, el buen mozo, es Jesús García.

BLOCK 5. On account of membership in a particular social group—PSG 1 proposed: Mexican drug lord/kingpin/smuggler/trafficker who was given status of confidential informant and subsequent protection by Mexican authorities.

D: *How did you come to the attention of the municipal police in Altar, Mr. García?*

R: Alguien **me requintó** con la Municipal, licenciado… no fue voluntario, no.

D: *Who accused you and of what?*

R: Nunca fui imputado por causa alguna, licenciado. No sé cómo terminaron mis datos en la Judicial; pero solo imagino que alguien habló más de la cuenta sobre mis negocios y mis asociados y así terminé en boca de la policía. Pero que quede claro, nunca me llegó orden de aprehensión en mi contra.

D: *What led to your entry in the Witness Protection Program, Mr. García López? Let's now talk about your entrance into the witness protection program. When did you start in the program, Mr. García López?*

R: El día que se conmemoró el natalicio del Benemérito de las Américas, Benito Juárez…

(IJ interrupts R, places his hands behind his nape and leans back on his chair.)

IJ: *LIMIT YOURSELF TO ANSWER THE QUESTION, MR. GARCÍA—MR. GARCÍA LÓPEZ!*

D: *And what date was that, Mr. García?*

R: Un día de asueto.

IJ: *Sir, do you recall the day and month when you started in the Witness Protection Program?*[27]

R: El veinte o veintiuno de marzo del año dos mil quince, dieciséis, ¿dieciséis? dieciséis, magistrado.

IJ: *Sir, in the year 2016?*

R: Pos sí, licenciado, así es señor.

D: *Mr. García, did anyone specifically explain to you about the kind of protection you were to receive and what that entailed under the Witness Protection Program?*

R: Añil, licenciado. El teniente Teobaldo Mata me lo dijo bien claro, él me informó que me protegerían de hasta amenazas, y

---

[27] Santos, Lic. G. Avila, Lic. P. (Enero de 2010). *Protección de testigos contra la delincuencia organizada.* Mexico: Centro de Documentación, Información y Análisis. Recuperado de http://www.diputados.gob.mx/sedia/sia/spe/SPE-ISS-01-10.pdf

por supuesto de ataques que pudiera sufrir. La protección incluía intento de homicidio y conminación. Me designaron testigo clave para que yo cooperara con su investigación de ellos, licenciados.

D: *Could you tell this court why were you specifically part of the Witness Protection Program, Mr. García López?*

R: ¡Va! En primer lugar porque la policía me quiso interrogar por la presunta afiliación con cárteles del narcotráfico.

(R pauses, scratches his forehead, then proceeds.)

R: Encima de eso les dije yo que me habían atacado en varias ocasiones. Les dije que fueron hombres armados, algunos enmascarados, y que no sabía si eran narcos o meros pandilleros.

(R pauses, smiles, then continues.)

R: Que entre nosotros y a decir verdad, no sabía yo si había sido la misma policía quien me había atacado, hay gente corrupta en la fuerza para que ustedes sepan; eso me empujó a yo convertirme en informante. A decir verdad, creo que no tuve otra. Muchos accidentes extraños ocurrieron que hicieron que mi vida comenzara a peligrar, así que no tuve otra que aceptar la propuesta de la Judicial del Municipio de Altar y hacerme soplón y acogerme a su protección.

D: *Did the municipal police in Altar give you any official status,*
Mr. García?

R: Como les dije y repito, me nombraron testigo clave... El
primer agente que me interrogó... creo que fue el teniente Mata,
me explicó que La Procuraduría General de la República y su
Procurador auspiciaban la protección de testigos... Usó palabras
grandotas el señor Mata.

D: *Did the category of key witness have any implications, Mr. García?*
What does it mean to become a key witness?

R: Llámeme Jesús Antonio García López o García López,
licenciado. ¡García es mi padre!

(R pauses, drinks water, then continues.)

R: Le explico, al convertirse uno en testigo clave, se le ofrece
protección y reserva de identidad con la idea de neutralizar
cualquier acoso o intimidación contra uno por manos de los
narcos. Los narcos van a luchar por impedir o frustrar la
indagatoria, entienda usted… Todo eso y mucho más me leyeron
en la Judicial, y bien que lo memoricé.

D: *Did you have to report or meet with anyone in particular at the judicial*
municipal police, Mr. García López?

R: Pos sí, licenciado.

D: *Who did you report to at the judicial municipal police, Mr. García López?*

R: Cada miércoles atravesado, me tenía que reportar con el agente PZ, así se hacía llamar. Oía que le llamaban PZ muchos cabos y tenientes que entraban y salían del despacho; incluso gendarmes de la Federal así le llamaban.

D: *What kind of level or rank did agent PZ hold in the municipal police, Mr. García?*

R: Era un agente, era un enlace, licenciado. No sé qué grado tendría el hombrín pues nunca se ponía uniforme.

D: *Mr. García López, are you aware of the different levels of the law enforcement in Altar?*

R: Bueno, hoy día sé que tienen el Mando Único Policial en el municipio de Altar…

(R ponders. D quickly looks down at a legal pad and interrupts R with a question.)

D: *Mr. García, Mr. García López, what is the Mando Único Policial, if you know?*

R: Son agentes de las fuerzas armadas, de la marina y de la policía estatal… son esos los que forman el Mando Único Policial.[28]

D: *So, did agent PZ belong to any of those forces, Mr. García López?*

R: No sabría decirle con exactitud, el vestía de civil, licenciado, pero su oficina radicaba en la Municipal.

D: *So, when you were accepted into the Witness Protection Program, what level of the Mexican police offered you protection, Mr. García López?*

R: La Judicial Municipal, aunque más tarde con la Gendarmería Nacional y en la medida que me inmiscuí más con mis asociados, después pasé a ser protegido de la mismísima Federal.

D: *By associates you mean narcotraffickers, Mr. García López, don't you?*

ACC: *Objection—leading question!*

IJ: *Sustained!*

D: *Who were your associates, Jesús?*

R: Los investigadores le llamaban por narcos, licenciado *Bollinger.*

---

[28]Secretaría de Seguridad y Protección Ciudadana. (11 de enero, 2014). La CNS atestiguó el abanderamiento del Mando Único Policial en Sonora. *Gobierno de México*. Recuperado de https://www.gob.mx/sspc/prensa/la-cns-atestiguo-el-abanderamiento-del-mando-unico-policial-en-sonora-162578

(R smiles and lowers and hides his head.)

D: *As a whistleblower, Mr. García López, what did you have to do?*

ACC: *Objection. Leading—*

IJ: *Sustained!*

D: *How often did you report with the police, Jesús?*

R: Pos, la policía municipal me dio información para compartir con mis contactos, con mis asociados, quiero decir, con los jefes, los gerentes que me relacionaba, en fin, con los individuos que hacía yo negocio jeta a jeta, que les digo cada vez eran más y más… A su vez, ellos me suministraban la información que les daba yo a la policía a cambio de protección. A la policía les informaba de cargamentos que mi gente planificaba, de **levantones**, que dicho sea de paso a veces eran verdaderos, otras veces era puro teatro. Como comprenderá, veía yo a mis asociados bastante a menudo… Mire usted, y para serles sincero, a veces yo les daba información, a la policía, sobre la **leperuza**, sobre pandillas chicas, grupúsculos que se forman a cada rato y competían con los grandotes… entonces la policía andaba como perros atrás de ellos, los perseguían, los atacaban y muchas veces los metían presos y hasta su juicio se les hacía. Sobre esas banditas yo sabía la información de sus **punteros, alijos** de narcóticos y laboratorios... me era fácil conocer donde tenían

sus *labs, meth labs, see?* A menudo los escondían entre la maleza de

los cerros y las cañadas. Los pequeñitos tenían que

desaparecer... entonces yo los soplaba, iban a desaparecer de

todos modos... muchos de ellos me debían plata, y no querían

soltar la plata... gente ingrata, hija de la gran puta... ¿Se imagina?

yo mismo les había montado sus negocios, pero se volvían

glotones y no me pagaban... pues vaya, ahí tenían su merecido...

no me costaba nada soplarlos de mi camino. Así mantenía

ocupado y hasta cierto punto distraído, a los de la Municipal, en

definitiva, algunos de ellos cooperaban con los *cartels*... aquello

era como un juego. Y recibía mi **lana** de ambas manos y

protección. Aquellos que me debían, si no pagaban, los soplaba.

D: *Why would you lie to the municipal police, Mr. García López?*

R: No podía causar sospecha a mis asociados, algunos

terminaban de gente grande y poderosa. Y me hubieran

asesinado de haberse olido una **fullería**, un engaño. Mi instinto

propio me decía que tenía que protegerme tanto de la Municipal

como de los asociados y sus cárteles. Además, la Municipal

perseguía a los **meros, meros**, a los jefes gordos, a los meros del

cártel, no a las raticas pandilleras, señores... de todos modos de las banditas me valía yo para pescar a los peces gordos… esa era mi estrategia para sobrevivir.

D: *Would it be fair to say that you were considered a bona fide informant?*

R: Sí, la Judicial del Municipio de Altar en Sonora me dio la categoría de testigo clave, colaborador, y me declaró categoría informante y ofreció protección personal.

D: *Did the protection include any other member of your family, Mr. García López?*

R: No, solo para Jesús Antonio García López, muy claramente lo advirtieron.

BLOCK 6. Threats. Altar Judicial Municipal Police.

D: *So, Mr. García López did the attacks stop as a consequence of your being protected by the local police? Were you* scared *at any point?*

ACC: *Objection!*

IJ: *Sustained!*

D: *I'll rephrase the question, Mr. García. Did the attacks stop?*

R: No creo, licenciado. ¿La protección? ¡Bah!

D: *Were you scared at any point?*

R: Claro. Era puro papeleo, muchas entrevistas, indagatorias, pero me sentí desamparado. ¡No era buena la protección! Miedo tuve, claro que sí.

(R pauses, looks around and behind him, then continues.)

R: Los ataques siguieron incluso contra mi hermanita Guadalupe. Los hijos de la gran puta comenzaron con asaltos del tipo solapados… a decir verdad… ella no tenía protección ninguna, ni colaboraba con la Judicial, pero no sé… no sé por qué la atacaban a ella.

D: *What, if anything, did your sister Guadalupe report to you, Mr. García López?*

R: Nada. Nunca me informó; ni tampoco fue a la policía; más tarde me enteré de los muchos asedios que sufrió, la pobre.

BLOCK 7. Threats and attacks. The disappearance of the Chihuahua of García López's sister Guadalupe.

D: *Do you recall when your sister was attacked for the first time, Mr. García López?*

R: No, no recuerdo y fueron muchísimos los ataques, pero como nunca me platicó… no sabía yo… Lo que sí resonó fue el incidente de la desaparición del **pinche** chihuahua de la Lupe.

Tendría que haber sido **de parte tarde** cuando sucedió.

IJ: *DO YOU RECALL THE DATE, MR. GARCÍA?*

R: Era el Día de Muertos.

D: *What happened to the pet, Mr. García López?*

(IJ cuts in, raising his voice again.)

IJ: *DO YOU RECALL THE EXACT DATE, SIR?*

R: Sí, el dos, el dos de noviembre…

IJ: *PROCEED, MR. BOLLINGER!*

D: *What happened to the pet, Mr. García López?*

R: Se robaron *el baby* de La Virgen, licenciado.

D: *Mr. García, you just mentioned La Virgen. Who is La Virgen,*
Mr. García López?

R: Así apodan a mi hermanita… La Santa… La Virgen,
licenciado.

D: *What's your sister's name, Mr. García López?*

R: Santa Gertrudis Guadalupe García López, licenciado.

D: *So, La Santa, La Virgen, La Lupe are the same person, Mr. García*
López?

R: Añil, licenciado. Cada quién le llamaba como le parecía, desde
que era **chava,** y así se le fueron quedando los apodos y

sobrenombres… De niña le llamaban la **coyota**, pero ese mote no se pegó… el de Santita y La Virgen fueron más populares.

(*R sheds a tear.*)

D: *So, your sister's pet was stolen—and then what happened, Mr. García López?*

R: Santita tenía mascotas de cada pretendiente o galanteador… tenía cotorras, un avestruz, un pavo real, un monito-ardilla, hasta un **zaino**… que dicho sea de paso, tenía que cuidárselo uno de mis **compas**, en su establo de Carnero. La Santita poseía un mini zoo… Santita se volvió una mujer ostentosa… A pesar de sus **bártulos de aturdida** conseguía lo que se pretendía… Era **viborona**.

D: *So, which of your sister's pets was the one that was stolen, Mr. García López?*

R: ¿La mascota? ¡Ah! La Cachorrita… ese era su **vuqui** y chaperona. Ella le llamaba La Cachorrita y desapareció, como le dije… Unas semanas más tarde, un **tata** la encontró, **luego luego** que Santita pusiera mantas de recompensa, en cada **tanichi** y regara la voz por **mentideros** de Altar y Carnero. El animalito finalmente apareció gracias a dios. El cuerpo del canino apareció

encobijado en una manta con garabatos, y una soga colgada del mismísimo cuello.

(R points at his nape.)

D: *When did Lupe's pet disappear, Mr. García López?*

R: La perrita desapareció más o menos alrededor del dos de noviembre, como le platiqué.

D: *Again, how is possible that you remember that date with such precision, Mr. García? And what year was it?*

(R snarls and mumbles a few words before responding.)

R: Porque era el Día de Muertos, licenciado. Si no mal recuerdo eso fue *in or around 2016.*

IJ: *WOULD YOU LIKE TO TESTIFY IN ENGLISH, SIR?*

R: Me disculpa, es puro nervio, su señoría…

(D interrupts R.)

D: *Then what happened, Mr. García?*

R: Lupe le dio santa sepultura a La Cachorrita…

(D interrupts R.)

D: *Now, you mentioned there was a **narcomanta** left next to Cachorrita's body. Do you recall what the flier said, Mr. García?*

R: No, licenciado, pero después que hallaron a la mascota, La Lupe me comentó de varias **narcomantas** que encontró clavadas en la puerta de su **chante**. **Luego luego** me dijo ella que una de las mantas decía, "Los chivos las pagan". ¡Ah! Al **zaino** lo vieron con sábanas a cada lado del cuerpo, el **zaino** galopeando, desbocado por medio de Altar, y la tela decía algo como, "Sapos policías brinquen **al otro lado**".

D: *Do you know why Santa Gertrudis never mentioned those facts to you or anyone else, Señor Jesús Antonio?*

R: La Virgen tuvo miedo o estuvo confundida. Estaría aterrorizada quizás, ¿Quién sabe? La Santa es muy llorona. ¿Cómo iba a saber ella en lo que yo andaba metido?

D: *Did that message in the **narcomanta** mean anything to you, Mr. García López?*

R: Sí, licenciado. Estaba clarito para mí. Los informantes, los soplones, pagan con la muerte, no hay otra explicación, licenciado. Y aquel mensaje no era para La Virgen, era para mí.

D: *Did Santa live with you?*

R: No, ella tenía su casón. Yo se lo hice a mano.

D: *Was your sister Guadalupe aware of your business or have any idea what you were involved with, Mr. García?*

R: ¿La Lupe? Ella vivía en los celajes, no levantaba una milpa, vivía para sus **menjurjes**, su figura, sus amistades y la **feria**, licenciado. Ella ni modo tuvo la menor idea de mi negocio, licenciado, y no creo que le importara. Si acaso, licenciado… ella pensó que yo **chambeaba** en la construcción y entrega de materiales. Ella me veía lidiando en el *business* de los caballos… a ella le gustaba montar, era buen jinete… Teniendo ella **feria**, era mujer contenta.

BLOCK 8. La Lupe's assassination. Shooting at Cerro Humo. Abduction and ransom.

D: *When did the next incident occur, Mr. García López?*

(R jots something down on a piece of paper, then reads from it.)

R: El doce de diciembre del año dos mil dieciséis, licenciado.

IJ: *How come you remember the date with such precision, sir?*

R: Pos, pasó el día que celebramos La Virgencita, señor.

IJ: *Which Virgen, sir?*

R: La Morena, licenciado. La patrona de México, magistrado.

IJ: *Do you know the name of the Virgen, sir?*

R: Esta virgencita que guardo junto a mi pecho, su señoría…

Guadalupe, su señoría.

D: *Was anything special happening that day in the town of Altar,*

Mr. García?

(R nods.)

IJ: *IS THAT A "YES," MR. GARCÍA?*

R: ¡**Añil**, licenciados! Teníamos la fiesta patronal religiosa en honor a La Reina, esto ocurre en el pueblo de Altar, los once y los doce del último mes del año.

D: *What happened on that date, Jesús?*

R: Estaba yo a la orilla de la acera... había acabado de pagar el **estacionómetro**... fumaba un **macuchi**... de repenete el agente PZ se metió en mi **charanga** y me tocó por el hombro derecho...

(IJ interrupts R.)

IJ: *HOW WAS AGENT PZ ABLE TO FIND YOU, MR. GARCÍA?*

(R clears his throat and stares at the interpreter.)

R: El Churro sabía que yo andaba con un grillete delator, en el tobillo. Así me encontraba. Él sabía que no podía escaparme así de fácil, licenciado.

D: *To clarify, Mr. García, who is El Churro?*

R: Era otro apodo del agente PZ. Escuché a cabos y soldados rasos de la Judicial llamarle así, incluso un mayor le gritó desde la puerta, "¡Churro, la pistola!". Yo escuché el mote durante una de las entrevistas... También recuerdo que el cabo Sancho, usaba el mote cuando le llevaba café al despacho... Sancho era el ayudante del Churro, y le decía: "Aquí tiene su cafecito, Churro". **Pos,** tendría confianza con su mero jefe.

D: *Now, how could you remember so vividly the date agent PZ got into your car, Mr. García?*

R: Era un miércoles atravesado, el día de la procesión de la Guadalupana, como ya les platiqué. Yo descansaba. No me hallaba bien de la cabeza. Tuvo que ser el segundo día de las fiestas patronales en honor a La Virgen, a La Virgen de Guadalupe.

D: *So, agent PZ got into your car, he touched you on your right shoulder— and did he say anything, did he utter any words so you could recognize him, Mr. García López?*

R: Sabía que era él, que era el PZ. El hedor lo delató. Él sacó su celular, me lo mostró y me susurró al oído, "Encontraron a La Santa, tu Lupe apareció en Potrero Semental, su cuerpo **jiruto**, violada y sin lengua".

(R pauses and sobs.)

D: *Now, did detective PZ give you any indication what happened in that pastureland, Mr. García?*

R: No, solo me enseñó las fotos y me dijo que en la opinión de los detectives el asesinato acababa de ocurrir.

D: *Did you in fact go to that farm looking for your relative's body?*

R: Fui **corriendito** a Potrero Semental. No había ni llegado, y ya de lejito se escuchaba una **bramona**… los animales estaban alebrestados, señor. Y cerca de la cochiquera estaba **testito de auras**… Entonces, me planto frente al **trochil**, a buscar y rebuscar… y en el corral, en la mera pocilga, vi un bulto. ¡**Caíta**! Ni sombra del cuerpo. Se lo habían llevado. "Me tardé", me dije.

D: *How far were you from Altar, Mr. García?*

R: El Potrero quedaba a media legua del pueblo.

D: *Once in the pigsty, did you hear any noise or smell anything?*

R: Olía a estiércol **pos** había **boñigas** por doquier. Aquella barbaridad me tenía mal de la cabeza.

D: *Share with this court how that* atrocity *made you feel, Mr. García López?*

R: En aquel momento me cayó una congoja muy fuerte. Sentí un golpe bajo, un golpe duro. Pensé en su **vuqui** que por suerte vivía en Aguas Prietas con Pancha, la hermana mayor.

D: *What, if anything, did you do next, Mr. García López?*

R: Pasé tres noches en el Humo, en el cerro Humo... allá la **pasé chopa**, medio **teporocho**. Comencé **dándome pericazos**. **Chupé mota**, también me **arponeé** anfetaminas y bebí hasta envenenarme la sangre, licenciado.

D: *And what happened after that, Mr. García?*

R: Desperté cubierto en vómito encima de la cama del Chapo.[29] Traté de incorporarme y pude ver que estaba en una **covacha** sin luz. El **tata**, el chamán octogenario apareció, y me dijo, "Vete al D.F. y comienza limpio".

D: *What did you do next, Mr. García López? Did you in fact go to el D.F.?*

(R points at his chest and remains silent, then cries.)

R: No, no, no nunca. Decidí regresar a Altar.

D: *Once you were in Altar, what happened, Mr. García López?*

R: Llegué a mi casa, subí a la recámara en el segundo piso y hallé el celular, casi sin carga, en la losa. El celular se había caído del colchón, al parecer, de tanto vibrar. Me distraje viendo el retrato de mi hermanita, el celular sonó una vez más. Contesté y una

---

[29] Ramos, J. (18 de diciembre, 2017). Premio Nacional de Artes a "Don Chapo." *Siempre!* Recuperado de http://www.siempre.mx/2017/12/premio-nacional-de-artes-a-don-chapo/

chica gritaba, "Ven Jesusito, ven a buscarme Jesusito, dales lo
que te pidan por Dios, te lo imploro Jesusito". El celular se
apagó y quedé petrificado como piedra, licenciado. Era la voz de
Lupe, mi hermanita Guadalupe resucitó o ¿era patraña,
licenciado?

D: *Was she alive or had she been* kidnapped, *Mr. García? What
happened, Jesús?*

R: La Santa estaba confinada, licenciado. Maleantes la tenían
presa por bocona, la habían secuestrado. Era un **desmadre**,
licenciado.

D: *What was the confusion about, Mr. García López?*

R: El agente PZ me mostró fotos, licenciado, yo vi un cuerpo,
licenciado… Este, este, este, mi hermanita estaba viva, nunca
murió, la habían raptado, licenciado. ¿A quién creer? ¿En quién
confiar en lo adelante?

D: *Did you know then who had kidnapped your beloved sister,
Mr. García?*

R: Ni modo. Dejé la cantidad que pedían, unos cien mil pesos
mexicanos… Yo salí al lugar indicado al siguiente día, y me la
entregaron en la iglesia del pueblo, en el mismito Altar. Yo seguí
las órdenes de los secuestradores, tal y como me instruyeron, en

una segunda llamada. La segunda vez, escuché la voz de una **chava**… ella no quiso identificarse.

IJ: *Sir, in your I-589, you didn't recount any of the stories you just told this court. Is there any reason why you didn't do so?*

R: **¡Ah pos!** No sé, la verdad que no sé por qué no está en esa planilla, su señoría.

(R looks at D and pauses, waiting for an answer from D, then resumes his testimony.)

R: Yo conté toda mi historia y más de la cuenta… Es la verdad, solo la verdad y nada más que la verdad, magistrado.

D: *Mr. García, where is your sister nowadays?*

R: En Aguas Prietas, en Sonora.

D: *What is she doing in Aguas Prietas, Mr. García?*

R: Casada, de ama de casa, de figurín, paseando, dándose lujos de señorona. No sé, La Virgen solo sabrá.

D: *Who did she marry, Mr. García?*

R: Un hombre de negocios, un **fondeado**.

D: *What kind of business, Mr. García?*

R: Un mero mero de Aguas Prietas. Un hombre poderoso, un narco, licenciado.

D: *Did you ever find out who abducted your sister Guadalupe, Mr. García López?*

R: ¿Entonces tenía o no razón yo para dudar de cada persona? Nunca supe si fue narco o policía quien raptó a La Lupe. Fue bien extraño ¿Verdad? **Nomás** pagué el rescate y La Santita se me fue de amoríos al norte, y terminó con el gandul de quien es hoy su esposo, amante... o ¿esposo? No sé... Por mucho tiempo no se habló del asunto, licenciado.

D: *I am going to ask you again, Mr. García. Did you ever find out who kidnapped or abducted Guadalupe?*

R: Ella misma. Fue un embrollo, una jugarreta, licenciado.

D: *For the sake of clarification, Mr. García, what do you mean by dirty trick?*

R: La Lupe y sus secuaces, quizás su maridito, pactaron el secuestro.

IJ: *How in the world did you find that out, Mr. García?*

R: Usted sabe cómo es la vida, magistrado, y como dice el refrán: Al nopal lo van a ver nomás cuando tiene tunas... Pancha me lo confesó... hace unos días. Pancha me andaba buscando para pedirme **feria**, a cambio de una confesión.

IJ: *Where's Pancha today, Mr. García?*

R: En Valdez, señor... en Alaska, su señoría.

IJ: *IN THE UNITED STATES, SIR?*

R: POS SÍ.

D: *After you rescued or got back your sister Guadalupe, what did you do, Mr. García López?*

R: Fui en búsqueda de los supuestos malhechores. Entienda, andaba engañado yo, andaba a ciegas. Entonces fui a confrontar a los supuestos sicarios, muchos de ellos eran mis meros asociados. El PZ había mentido, **soltando un borreguero** aquella tarde, burlándose de mi lealtad e ignorancia.

D: *How do you know PZ was lying to you?*

R: Sacando cuenta, y aún no es certeza, pero el maridito de La Lupe era un narco asociado del PZ. ¿Se da cuenta, licenciado? ¿En quién creer?

D: *What's his name, Jesús?*

R: Alias El Cristal, pero su nombre completo es Narciso Piedra.

BLOCK 9. Threat. Warning by Gaviota.

D: *Who did you go after, Mr. García?*

R: Los hijos de la chingada madre, Gaviota y Chavito, señor.

IJ: *SIR, WHO ARE THOSE INDIVIDUALS?*

R: Dos de mis asociados, su señoría.

D: *If anything, what did Gaviota and Chavito tell you about your sister's disappearance, Mr. García López?*

R: "Pura casualidad", así dijeron. "Vete a ver con quién anda La Virgen", me dijo Gaviota. Así le llamaban ellos a mi hermanita. Ella era independiente y no quería amoríos con nadie o con ninguno de los hombres del Gaviota; pero se sabía que era bien coqueta la hermanita. Gaviota también me amenazó diciéndome, "Cuídate las espaldas Caraebarbie".

BLOCK 10. Sabotage against Naranjita, Mr. García López's pickup truck.

D: *So, what happened next, Mr. García?*

R: Quemaron mi **troca** naranja, una *RAM Big Horn*, con solo quince mil seiscientos cincuenta y cuatro millas. Mi gran **pick up** señor, con cristales polarizados, una preciosura, licenciados.

D: *How did you find out about it, Mr. García?*

R: Un ayudante vino a avisarme que había visto a unos tres o cinco hombres quemando la Naranjita. La habían visto cuneta abajo, a la salida del barrio Bella Vista al norte de Altar. **Mi cuate** me dijo que se olía a petróleo a una milla de donde la abandonaron, después de achicharrarla. Mi **cuate**, El Tapón, vio la **troca** arder, licenciado.

D: *When did that happen, Mr. García?*

R: Tuvo que ser entre el doce al quince de diciembre, licenciado.

D: *2016?*

R: Pos sí, dos mil dieciséis, *2016.*

D: *Did they leave any messages, any sign as to who could have done it?*

R: ¿Señal? La **troca** la saquearon... uno de mis choferes dejó la llave dentro y fue a tomar un **atole**... al regresar ni rastro de mercancía, y la **ranfla** ardía… Extraño fue que el berraco no oyó la explosión, que por el contrario cualquiera hubiera escuchado *in Yuma.*

IJ: *IN YUMA?*

(IJ cackles.)

D: *What kind of merchandise were you carrying in the truck, Mr. García?*

R: Puro pirotecnia, unas cuarenta cajas de fuegos artificiales, cajas con petardos, sacos de pólvora, cohetes de señales, morteros de luces, cañas voladoras, envases con varias químicas. Era un encargo para *party* de fin de año de uno de mis asociados. Por eso es extraño que nadie oyó nadita.

D: *Did you report that to the municipal police?*

R: Sí señor. Al cabo Sancho le informé, en la ausencia del penco, **mamón** de PZ.

BLOCK 11. Narco-blankets. Mines, weapons, recruitment. Crime in the mine: El Águila kills Mota.

D: *Now, Mr. García López, as a key witness you continued working with your associates or those businesspeople you were connected with. Did the work you did for them change in anyway?*

R: Sí, un poco, licenciado

D: *So, could you tell this court what type of work you began doing or added to your line of work for your associates, Mr. García López?*

R: Tenía personal que colgaba mantas desde puentes, esos que cruzan autopistas, así los mensajes se hacían requetebién visibles. Tenía **chavos** que repartían folletos, otros reclutaban personal para varias organizaciones. Yo también organizaba la compra de tiradas completas de titulares, en periódicos... con reportes favorables o entrevistas sobre empresarios claves. El narco controla la prensa, sepa usted.

D: *Who hired you to do that?*

R: Los encargos venían solo de empresarios de Sonora.

D: *Did you do that before getting into the Witness Protection Program,*
Mr. García?

R: Nadie me pidió que hiciera semejante cosa; sin embargo, con mi entrada en el programa, mis nuevos asociados me comprometieron en actividades que antes nunca hice.

IJ: *What do you mean by associates, Mr. García?*

R: La Judicial y los hombres de negocios…

(D interrupts R.)

D: *How did they know you could do such work?*

R: Se los ofrecía, licenciado… era parte de la **chamba**, punto. Si me piden servicios, se ofrece el servicio… Se daba la **chanza** y cumplía con los encarguitos: así ganaba mi **lana**. Como informante, yo me informaba. Yo leía la prensa, estaba al tanto del mundo del ampa y lo que se necesitaba.

D: *Could you give us examples of what a given poster would say,*
Mr. García López?

R: **Añil**, licenciado, por ejemplo, El Grupo Operativo Pacífico Ltd necesita tu mano, se necesita soldado activo o guardias para cuerpo de seguridad privada, buena paga. Así decían, licenciado… También puse mantas para reclutar gente en Pótam, Vícam, Tórim, Bácum, Cócorit y Rahum. Como les dije, las colgaban en los cruces y puentes de autopistas de los pueblos que mencioné y muchos otros que **ahorita** no recuerdo.

D: *Why would they want soldiers or security guards, Mr. García?*

R: Los vigilantes profesionales tienen entrenamiento en armas de fuego, saben cargar y descargar armamento, limpiarlo, y preservarlo. Ese personal practica las artes marciales, defensa personal; son individuos físicamente aptos para pelear y defender a sus patrones y sitios claves. Son gente con experiencia en seguridad. No hay que pagar por entrenamiento señor.

D: *Have you ever been a security guard, Mr. García?*

R: Tres meses y algo, en la mina.

IJ: *THIS IS INTERESTING, ISN'T IT, MR. BOLLINGER?*

D: *Indeed, Your Honor. Mr. García, when did you start working in the mine?*

R: Mientras trabajaba para los túneles y después de que naciera mi primer hijo… necesitaba plata señor… así que tuvo que ser cuando tenía yo… veintitrés o veinticuatro años.

IJ: *What kind of mine was that, sir?*

R: Puro oro, oro de veinticuatro quilates se decía, magistrado.

D: *Where was that mine located?*

R: En Mulatos, Sahuaripa.

D: *Did you carry a weapon, Mr. García, as part of your job, I mean?*

R: Tenía un bastón expandible y un revólver calibre 38 SPL de cuatro pulgadas. Había quienes llevaban pistolas semiautomáticas, 9 mm, más bien para guardaespaldas de gerentes. También teníamos acceso a cuchillos, pero nunca los usé. Había postas que portaban escopetas calibre 12/70, eran armas reglamentarias según nos informó el jefe de armeros.

D: *Why did you leave that job after three months, Mr. García?*

R: Hubo un accidente… querían culparme y me salí.

IJ: *Did you kill anyone while working as a security guard, Mr. García?*

R: ¡No! El malhechor fue otro vigilante, El Águila… el tipejo era sobrino del armero… nos llamaban los gemelos, creo que por eso me buscaban a mí, para llevarme al penal. El Mota en medio de una práctica, le sacó el ojo al Águila, y este en represalia lo mató.

D: *Did you work as a security guard for any other company, residential complex or private individuals, Mr. García?*

R: Sí, en la mina La India, una mina canadiense, pero me fui… después que asaltaron y robaron la mina huí… Fueron hombres en pasamontañas… estaban encapuchados y armados de pies a cabeza… **Luego luego** me acusaron de complicidad con los malhechores… dijeron que los agresores estaban en complicidad con los guardias, con los vigilantes como yo, a pesar de que acribillaron a balazos a dos de las postas, mis compañeros, mis **cuates**. ¿Cómo pudieron acusarnos a los guardias de tal fechoría?

D: *Later on, after leaving the work in the mines, did you personally recruit anyone, Mr. García López?*

R: No personalmente, pero sabía con quién platicar para que otras personas buscaran los hombres que se necesitaban. Yo conocía a un **carajal** de gente y estaba en contacto con gente que manejaba brigadas de obreros, demoledores, carpinteros, soldadores, mozas de limpieza y empresas de vigilantes. La gente siempre me buscó para trabajar.

BLOCK 12. Narco-blanket's job. Jesús, the target.

D: *Your Honor, I am turning now to Exhibit 20, in Tab S, on page 33. It shows a narco-blanket that apparently bears the name of the respondent almost at the bottom of it. I'll hand it to the interpreter so she can sight-translate it. And my apologies beforehand because my Spanish is not that good, but it reads, "Pinche güerito. Zángano Caraebarbie. Donde quiera te* *arrancamos la lengua, por sapo. Nos vemos en el cerro. Atentamente: La*

Raza".

(The interpreter holds Exhibit 20 in her hands, takes a minute to read it,

then delivers the translation of the document.)[30]

D: *Do you recognize this message, Mr. García? When did you spot it and*

where were you living at the time, Mr. García López?

ACC: *Objection!*

IJ: *What is your objection, Ms. López?*

ACC: *I didn't hear the name of the respondent mentioned in Exhibit 20.*

This in no way, shape or form indicates that **narcomanta** *refers to the*

respondent. Wouldn't you agree, Mr. Bollinger?

D: *We already agreed that the respondent's alias is El Güero, as well as*

Caraebarbie, which was printed on that intimidating sheet. Wouldn't you

agree, Ms. López?

(R raises his hand.)

ACC: *NO! NOT GÜERITO! NOT A SINGLE TIME HAS*

MR. GARCÍA SAID THAT HE'S KNOWN AS GÜERITO!

(ACC pauses to read the exhibit.)

---

[30] Suggested translation: *"Goddamned little blond. Dumbass
Caraebarbie. For being a snitch, wherever we find you, we will rip out your
tongue. We'll see you on the mountain. Attentively, La Raza."*

ACC: *And I am looking at the exhibit in question, and the spelling is in lowercase letters, so it is used as an adjective that could be used to refer to any other person.*

D: *For heaven's sake, his name is at the bottom of the* **narcomanta***!*

IJ: *I'll allow it. Sir, answer the question please!*

R: ¡**Añil**, magistrado! Vi el mensajito, vi la **lona** con mis apodos. Como dice la agente del Ministerio Público, la licenciada López, mis enemigos me llamaban El Güerito para apocarme… Y es cierto que yo vi la **lona** que colgaba del cruce Periférico, allá en la Avenida Álvaro Obregón y General Ignacio Pesqueira. Me di cuenta cuando regresé de **Hermosío** al pueblo Altar, recuerdo haberle hecho retratos y guardarle. Lo tengo de recuerdo. Fue una advertencia más que me andaban persiguiendo, licenciados.

D: *Who was looking for you, Mr. García? Who could have been after you and why?*

R: El ampa, licenciado, mis enemigos, la policía, los envidiosos, los narcos; pero ¿qué facción? ¿quiénes? No sabía.

D: *Jesús, let me show you what has been identified and introduced as Exhibit 21, a picture with a similar message that bears the name Jesús. (The bailiff hands the picture to R.)*

D: *Is that a menacing message against you, Mr. García?*

R: *Sí, Jesús is my name, and my name is in that* **narcomanta.**

D: *Did you or the groups you worked for use posters or narco-blankets to intimidate rival factions, Mr. García?*

R: ¡Era la **fajina**, licenciado! Era la tarea encomendada… ¡sí!

D: *By the cartels?*

R: Yo cumplí órdenes.

D: *Who wrote the graphics, Mr. García?*

R: Imprentas locales… Yo recibo la pedida y yo mando a **chavos** que vayan por el encargo. Las imprentas se encargan de redactar las notas, las imprimen, después los **chavos** las cuelgan desde donde yo les pido.

D: *Why didn't you write them, Mr. García López?*

R: No soy ducho en eso de escribir, licenciado.

IJ: *Sir, could you give us an example of those retaliatory or confrontational messages you were asked to write, print and hang?*

R: Recuerdo que el señor Zapata siempre pedía escribir el mismo mensaje a soplones. Solo cambiaba los nombres para cada nuevo encargo. Algo que decía como así, "Pancho, **pinche** soplón, monta gallinas, cuelgas mantas para que la DEA te llene los bolsillos. Te vamos a sacar la lengua y las alas de un tajo. Vas a quedar **nacabochi**, puto. ATT: Mocho".

D: *What did you think about that message, Mr. García López?*

R: Daban miedo, pero no les prestaba atención, licenciado porque no eran contra mí. Recibía muchos pedidos de mantas, algunos eran bromas pesadas; aunque la mayoría iban en serio. Recuerdo que el mismo Zapata encargaba mantas para declarar su amor a varias **morras**, y aquellas **mantas** se pusieron en puentes cruzando la autopista por donde supuestamente cruzaba la homenajeada. Yo no prestaba atención a la escritura de cada manta, licenciado.

D: *Did Mr. Zapata ever kill any of those he threatened?*

R: Era un capo y lo que pedía, lo cumplían sus hombres. **Pos** si pidió que mataran, mataron.

D: *If you know, Mr. García, when you lived in the municipality of Altar, in the state of Sonora, was there a drug cartel that controlled the area, Mr. García López?*

R: No existe un cártel como tal en Sonora, no conozco cártel que se llame, El Cártel de Sonora, tampoco. Según escuché la DEA acabó con el más viejo de los cárteles del estado; aunque quedan sus líderes por ahí. Algunos que se creen meros buchones viven en **Hermosío** y en Aguas Prietas definitivamente viven allí; pero los **meros**, **meros** se aliaron al

Cártel de Tijuana y al de Sinaloa. Entonces los que quedan en Sonora andan dando vueltas, haciendo de las suyas queriendo ser los meros **mainates**. Nadie es bobo, licenciado… Eso sí, cuando hay oportunidad para ganar territorio y plazas, ellos hacen sus movidas y controlan los territorios.

BLOCK 13. On account of membership in a particular social group—PSG 2 proposed: Mexican drug lord/smuggler/trafficker who was given protection by a government entity, the local police and was working with cartels and instrumental in defying those cartels. Liaison.

D: *You mentioned you served as a liaison for different businessmen, important business owners, men with lots of dough in different sectors that needed your services, right, Mr. García?*

R: Añil señor. No hay nada que ocultar… Ya me lo han preguntado varias veces, millones de gente… Es la verdad, solo la verdad, y nada más que la verdad. Se lo juro, licenciado.

D: *What kinds of jobs are we referring to, Mr. García López? Would you mind telling us again?*

R: Bueno, bueno, yo busqué maestro de obras para sus construcciones de ellos, coordiné poner anuncios en el periódico

El Sonorense... el pobre quebró... el periódico quise decir...

También coordiné el envío de comunicados a redacciones de

prensa... Llamé a periodistas para que hicieran reportajes, de

modo que la policía se aparecía cuando había muertos en cunetas

o en la calle, cerca de los negocios de la competencia... También

se me pedía que dejara mensajes informando sobre testigos

oculares de balaceras, incendios, desaparecidos... También se

hacía un montaje en la supuesta escena del hecho: se dejaban

cuerpos, autos con placa comprometedoras, se dejaban ciertos

armamentos, así se hacía. Mis enlaces decían que así se le ganaba

a la competencia. Y no podía faltar, y como ya usted sabe,

mandaba a poner lonas amenazantes por todas partes.

D: *Did you order anyone to be killed?*

R: No, era solo un montaje, como les platiqué. La idea era que la

policía y periódicos le hicieran la vida imposible a la

competencia, como les platiqué, señores y señoras.

D: *Did you do any other jobs for your associates in El Grupo Operativo*

Pacífico Ltd, Mr. García?

R: Mandé reclutar hombres y los preparé como **punteros** y

halcones en las Sierras de *Arizona* para que movieran sus

mercancías. La sierra era una plaza importante para el tráfico...

Los **meros, meros** movían su cargo al mayoreo por aquella zona, ellos no eran como los **pinches** drogadictos que para mantener el vicio la mueven al menudeo.

D: *What kind of goods are you referring to, Mr. García López?*

R: Mercadería señor… No sé exactamente, pero El Grupo Operativo Pacífico Ltd, eran mercaderes al mayoreo, eran negociantes, dueños de muchos negocios, exportaban e importaban mercancías, movían contenedores, los meros grandes, *the 40 footers?* ¡Eso! Entonces se hace contrabando de todo señor… se trafica, se mueve todo tipo de drogas, artículos de consumo, frutas, avocados, de todo, licenciado, todo. Hasta ahí llegaba mi responsabilidad.

D: *Did you know the content of the merchandise, sir?*

R: *Oh no!*

IJ: *Did you ever inspect the merchandise?*

R: *Never!*

D: *Did you ever help in covert operations or retaliatory operations against other groups or any cartels or gangs in the state of Sonora, Mr. García López?*

R: Yo soy puro pacífico, licenciado. Esa no fue nunca mi **chamba**. Si acaso mariachi, pero ni sicario ni matón. Yo era el enlace.

(IJ interrupts.)

IJ: *FIVE MINUTES' RECESS!*

BLOCK 14. Threats and sabotage perpetrated as a result of informant job. Flashback: La Lupe's abduction. Rancho Los Güeros. Shooting weapons in the Cerro. Olive-green pickup truck on fire.

D: *So, could you tell us if you suffered any injuries? Or did anyone harm you or threaten you in relation to the informant job you were doing, Mr. García López?*

R: Le dije que quemaron mis **trocas**, raptaron a mi hermana… ¿Qué más?

ACC: *Objection! Abduction, Mr. Bollinger?*

IJ: *What's the basis for your objection, Ms. López?*

ACC: *It's known that the respondent is aware that his sister was never kidnapped.*

D: *We're not 100 percent sure she wasn't. Mr. García López received information from his sister, whose first and main interest was money. So we* *couldn't confirm whether in fact Santa Gertrudis García López was*

kidnapped or not. So let's assume she was.

ACC: *Bogus—speculative, to say the least!*

IJ: *LET THE RESPONDENT TELL HIS STORY!*

ACC: *But Your Honor, the respondent said, and he's under oath, that Santita wasn't abducted, and I quote: "Fue un embrollo, una jugarreta, licenciado".*

IJ: *I'll allow his testimony* nonetheless. *Sir, proceed. Mr. García, continue with your testimony please!*

R: Como dije, malhechores colgaron mantas en la casa de Santa Gertrudis, desmembraron al chihuahua, se robaron el caballo negro y a otras mascotas…

(D interrupts R.)

D: *As a result of all the attacks and threats against you and your sister, did you do anything, Mr. García López?*

R: La situación ya se ponía fea, licenciado y la Judicial no actuaba, entonces me dije, "¿venganza o huída?". Quizás mis enlaces estaban avisados de que cooperaba con rivales, con los del Pacífico, con **Hermosío**, con los de Aguas Prietas, ¿quién sabe? Entonces me fui al Rancho Los Güeros a recoger **lana** que me debían, y a averiguar qué estaba pasando.

D: *Did you in fact visit Rancho Los Güeros?*

R: ¡Sí! Yo crucé los doscientos kilómetros que separan Santa Gertrudis de Altar de **Hermosío**.

D: *And what happened once you reached the house, if anything?*

R: Llegué al Rancho y fue El Güero Gallito quien me recibió; él me dijo que no sabía de la desaparición de mi hermana Lupe... **Luego luego** me dijo que estaba muy apenado sabiendo cuánto yo la quería. Yo no mencioné nada sobre el rescate... Conversamos un rato, y nos dimos unos tequilas, eso así lo recuerdo. Los gemelos me sirvieron un menú de drogas, me invitaron, pero no acepté. Ya al final de la plática, tanto El Güero Buchón como su gemelo se disculparon una vez más por la pérdida de mi Santa, incluso ofrecieron recompensa por la captura de los sicarios.

D: *And then what happened, Mr. García?*

R: Extraño fue que mi **troca** no quería arrancar, una vez que anuncié mi partida. Suceso extraño ¿Eh? **Pos**, era una **troca** nueva. Entonces tuve que dejar la **troca** en su garaje, y fue El Güero Gallito quien me dio un aventón hasta la casa de un compa chapista, El Pollo. A él le daba yo mucho negocio, y como tenía uno de sus talleres en el centro de **Hermosío**, a su

taller llegué. Allí me prestó una **ranfla**. De allí, y **luego luego** de
unos tequilazos visité al señor Manzo; recogí una plata que me
debía y… Se me olvidaba, **luego luego** de platicar, le pedí razón
del secuestro de Santita; tampoco conseguí respuesta…

Entonces se hacía la **oscurana** y un ventarrón de tierra anunció
tormenta y partí. No quería que me agarrara la noche en la
carretera, entonces **me recalé** a mi colonia en Altar…

(IJ interrupts R.)

IJ: *Sir, if I am not mistaken, in your application you mentioned an Audi. I
believe you stated you onwed a yellowish Audi?*

R: No recuerdo, su señoría. Tuve un *R8 Spyder*, pero casi no lo
manejaba. Me lo robaron o lo cambié por otro, **ahorita** no
recuerdo.

IJ: *PROCEED, MR. BOLLINGER!*

D: *Was there any other incident or assault and battery perpetrated against
you in Altar or Hermosillo that we're not aware of or that you haven't
described this morning, Mr. García?*

R: No creo, solo recuerdo que al llegar a Altar, me monté en El
Diablo Rojo, era mi favorito **picapón**, y la noche la pasé en el
cerro disparando con calibre pesado. Recuerdo haberme llevado
un cuerno de chivo americano, una lanza granadas de 40 mm de

Sudáfrica y un par de pistolas alemana Heckler & Koch P7. De noche era bien **pinche** tirar salvas, licenciado. De noche no te molestan. Sí recuerdo bien que era domingo veinticuatro de diciembre, la **troca** verde olivo había cogido fuego, a la luz del día, y las tres tuercas y los dos tornillos que quedaron, se los llevaron al **deshuesadero** para máquinas de repuesto.

D: *How did you find out about it, Mr. García?*

R: La **troca** verde olivo estaba en el taller de Bujía, fui a buscarla y los mecánicos me comentaron que habían saboteado la planta. Nadie vio ni un **huotepoli** entrar al taller y perpetrar el incendio. Bujía, el dueño, me dijo que podrían reconstruir la **troca** usando una recién chocada; ellos las reconstruyen y las ponen a correr de la noche a la mañana. Le dije que lo olvidara. Era obvio que aquel acto era pura retaliación en coordinación con los mecánicos y su jefe, el mismísimo **pinche** Bujía.

D: *Did you report that occurrence to the police, Mr. García López?*

R: Reporté, sí que lo reporté, licenciado.

D: *Did the police do anything?*

R: Ellos no daban parte de nada, licenciado. Ellos viven ocupados en sus negocios, y pescando el peje gordo.

D: *Then what did you do, Mr. García López?*

R: Seguí recogiendo **feria**, licenciado.

D: *Was there any other assault or vandalism you suffered during that time as a result of your work as an informant, Mr. García?*

R: Así es.

D: *Did any other fires, holdups or assaults occur in which you were the target?*

R: ¡**Añil**, licenciado! Como le platiqué, antes de largarme de Sonora tenía que recoger plata que andaba suelta en la calle, y me costó cara recogerla.

BLOCK 15. Anecdote, Rancho Elote: Kawis, Gaviota and Chavito.

D: *Okay, what did you do then, Mr. García? Can you explain?*

R: Don **Kawis**… a **Kawis**, el viejo **ópata**, le alquilé su **charanga**. El hijoeputa… Íbamos rumbo al norte, a Nogales México. Ya Gaviota y Chavito estaban avisados que pasaría a recoger mi **lana**… Al llegar al rancho me esperaba una caja hecha de palo fiero, con todita la plata.

D: *Did anything happen to you while in Rancho Elote, Mr. García?*

R: Nada. Pero de vuelta del Elote, del rancho Elote, el **tata** entró en una aldea poblada por **chinamen**, a ambos lados de la angosta carretera… el **tata** habría manejado unos cinco o diez

minutos a lo sumo, y se oía una **chamuchina** gritando a ambos

lados, los chamacos jugaban en la cuneta… los **vuquis** nos

distrajeron con su jolgorio y chifladera, recuerdo que los

muchachos les hacían señas al **tata** para que tocara el claxon.

Cuando **recalé** la vista al **wipers** vi un retén de unos cinco o

siete hombres vestidos de civil. En la medida en que el

chingado aquel… el **Kawis,** se acercaba a la muchedumbre

notaba más y más tipejos portando fusiles de varios calibres. El

que se distinguía era un gringo alto y robusto con un cuerno de

chivo AK-47, apuntándonos.

D: *Were they Federales?*

R: Unos cuantos tenían uniformes con emblema "POLICÍA

MUNICIPAL", en el pecho. ¡**Vóytelas**! Tres enmascarados

saltaron de un arbusto plantado al borde del tramo de carretera

por la que transitábamos. Me sorprendieron, de veras.

D: *Did these uniformed persons shout or say anything?*

R: No, el hijo de mil putas, el **tata** paró la **charanga,** y los

enmascarados abrieron mi puerta de un tirón. Me jalaron y me

sacaron del taxi, jalándome y jalándome duro, por las piernas. ¡Se

armó un embrollo tremendo! Entonces, al caer yo a la carretera, un militar me pateó el trasero, mientras otro me golpeaba con la cacha de su rifle por el cuerpo. De un soplón, caí en la carretera, raspando mi jeta con el pavimento. Allí sentí el sabor a sangre en mis labios. **Y ¡riata!** Uno de los **vuquis** que jugaba en la cuneta me pateó la cabeza como si fuera una pelota de *soccer*. Acto y seguido recibí una lluvia de patadas en la espalda y piernas, y me dejaron irme de bruces cuneta abajo a la **acequia**.

D: *Did you hear any other noise or screams?*

R: Sentí disparos, un rat-tat-tat como de calibre pesado… un **triquitrate**… metralla viva, licenciado… como si estuvieran acribillando a alguien a puro tiro. Creí que habían despachado **al tata**… **Luego lueguito** los proyectiles silbaban encima de mi cabeza, yo seguía tendido en el canal. Los **capsules**, los casquillos de balas los veía caer bien cerquita de mi cuerpo.

(R grabs a plastic cup in front of him and drinks water.)

D: *Did they say anything while they were beating you, Mr. García López?*

R: ¡Claro! Mientras me pisoteaban oía carcajadas, burlas y, y, y hasta insultos… gritaron hasta desmadrarse: "**Pinche** chivato… te enterramos vivo, lengualarga… no escarmientas puto. ¿A quién sirves soplón? Sapo… puto **güero**". **Luego luego** me voltearon como carnero. Ahora me pateaban en la panza y la sangre seguía saliendo a chorros por la boca. Perdí el conocimiento. Quedé con la cara achatada y un costurón, una cicatriz en la frente es testimonio. Mire, mire usted... **Ahorita** dependo de **antiparras** para leer la prensa.

(R points at his forehead.)

D: *Who do you blame for the ambush?*

R: Al viejo **Kawis**... El **tata** se salió con la suya, salió ganando, **se enchalecó mi lana**. El tipejo se quedó con el botín, licenciado.

D: *Who kicked you, Mr. García?*

R: Vi a un hombre fornido, gordo, **güero** el hombrín.

(R gestures and stands up, attempting to illustrate the size of the man he referred to.)

Bailiff: *Sit down, sir!*

D: *How tall or big was the blond man?*

R: Ah no recuerdo, quizás siete pies y trescientas libras, grande el hombrín, parecía un futbolista. Parecía **un yori** de la DEA, licenciado.

D: *What was this seven foot-tall, three hundred-pound man doing to you, Mr. García?*

R: *Kicking, he kicked* mi cara y estómago, licenciado... Parecía **cúmaro**.

D: *While the seven-foot, three hundred-pound blond was kicking your abdomen and face, where was* **Kawis?**

R: ¡Ah! **Pos,** fíjese que no recuerdo, señor *Bollinger*.

D: *Again, Mr. García, when did the attack take place?*

R: A fines del dos mil dieciséis.

D: *Thank you, Jesús.*

BLOCK 16. Hospital General de Caborca. Threats: narco-blanket at the door.

D: *Did anything happen to the taxi driver, Mr. García López?*

R: Ni pizca señor. Probablemente al **cacalbro** lo querían para devolverme a casa.

D: *Where did you go after they beat you up and left you unconscious, Mr. García López?*

R: El octogenario me llevó a una clínica, mejor dicho, a un hospital, al Hospital General de Caborca, y más nunca supe del viejo. En el hospital me cosieron, me entablaron, me limpiaron las orejas, me habían taponeado las orejas con lodo, licenciado.

D: *Did they leave any threatening or intimidating notes with the old cabdriver, Mr. García López?*

R: Encontraron una manta en el portón de mi hacienda, la manta que clavaron, leía: "Puto Policía. Tienes tu sentencia: MUERTE". También saqueron mi **cantón**. No dejaron ni **bejo'orim** en mi jardín. Saquearon la hacienda y destruyeron plantas y árboles…

(D interrupts R.)

D: *How did you find out about it, Mr. García?*

R: Mecha me dijo.

D: *For clarification's sake, Mr. García López, who is Mecha?*

R: Ella era mi empleada, era moza de limpieza, quedó embarazada, y hoy es madre de mi hija Lupe.

IJ: *Mr. García, it sounds as though you've been through a lot in such a short time and we've been conducting the hearing for two hours now. Do you need a longer recess?*

R: ¡**Va!** y **pos sí**, magistrado. Que lo diga usted, sí que consta. A mí también pues hace falta tomarme un Café de Talega.

Recess during direct examination (break for the interpreter)

BLOCK 17. Anecdote: Incident at Rancho Elote with Gaviota and Chavito.

D: *Mr. García, let's go back and talk about the facts that occurred on February 6, 2017. What happened that day?*

R: Me encaminé al rancho Elote, tenía que devolverle la visita al **pochi** Marcos y a su amigacho Harry, aliases Chavito y Gaviota. Para llegarme al rancho había alquilado una ambulancia del Hospital Caborca. Al llegar a Elote, desde las rejas alguien gritó, "¿qué vamos a hacer contigo Caraebarbie?". Escuché tipejos abuchando sandeces ahí, desde dentro del casón: "No sirves para nada zorrillo". Una de las voces me sonaba al **pinchi zorrastrón** de Chavito. De pronto, se apareció uno de sus hombres, él se parapetó en el portalón de la mansión, desenfundó una Glock enchapada en oro, y no tuve otra que dispararle. Al tipejo le abrí un hueco entre ceja y ceja, licenciado.

D: *Did Gaviota show up, Mr. García?*

R: Luego lueguito uno muy parecido a Gaviota surgió en bata de baño, con una sonrisa burlona y una botella de **bacanora** en su mano derecha. Estaba él en la terraza, sepa usted, y tenía yo el sol frente a la cara así que no distinguía bien, pero estaba seguro de que era Gaviota. El **pochi** gritó en inglés unos disparates ahí, algo así como que me saliera del negocio, y yo le contesté, "No

Gaviota, aquí el único hombre en pie soy yo". Él entonces gritó,

"Go to hell Caraebarbie." Yo le pregunté, "¿Quién raptó a la

Lupe?". El hombrín no paraba de burlarse, y finalmente gritó,

"Agarra la plata, móntate en el burro, y piérdete cabrón, antes

que me arrepienta".

D: *What did these words mean to you, Mr. García?*

R: No sé, pero era obvio que me habían hecho una trastada,

licenciado. La primera entrega de plata que hicieron era falsa.

Solo los billetes de encima de la caja eran fidedignos, y se los

había entregado yo a la enfermera que me atendió en el hospital.

Era mucha plata, el resto de la **lana** era falsa, licenciado. Me

habían engañado, licenciado. ¿Cuál era su plan entonces?

¡Querían que regresara para ajusticiarme! ¿No cree usted?

D: *Do you know what he meant by all the things he said? I mean Gaviota?*

R: ¡**Nel**, licenciado! Como le digo, no sé, pero cierto es que, en

este negocio, se juega al duro y sin guantes. Yo les tiré duro,

licenciado. Yo apreté el gatillo de mi arma y se armó una balacera

fugaz, a un Gaviota vi caer al suelo, arriba en la terraza. La

botella del mezcal le cayó encima, y un fuego le cubrió. Vaya

manera de **clavar el pico** el chacal, creí yo entonces, licenciado.

Luego luego me sacaron a patadas de la hacienda… fueron los guardaespaldas que me sacaron.

D: *Obviously the guards didn't kill you. Why do you think that was, Mr. García?*

R: Pos, estuve más trocado que antes. "Pura casualidad", pensé yo. La cosa es que vivo me dejaron… Este negocio es un quítate tú para ponerme yo, licenciado; pero si me dejaron vivo, la razón debe de ser porque los jefes gordos me necesitaban. No me querían perder. ¿Qué otra **babosada** hubiera podido ser?

D: *Did you suffer any injuries as a result of the gunshots, any gunshot wounds or from gunfire?*

R: Como le dije a su secretaria, me dispararon a las canillas, a las piernas y muslos, tengo cicatriz para probárselo. No caminé por mucho tiempo, **nel**.

IJ: *Did you talk to anyone about this incident, Mr. García?*

(R sobs and remains quiet.)

BLOCK 18. Protection house: Altar. Comandante Moreno. Transfer to Hermosillo protection house: La Mazmorra.

D: *Mr. García—sir—Mr. García, did you discuss what transpired at Rancho Elote with anyone?*

R: En la casa de protección hablé con el señor Moreno, el comandante Moreno. Un hombre muy serio. Al despertar la primera mañana, pensé yo estar en una clínica de rehabilitación, pero al ver tanta seguridad, policías, gente uniformada que entraba y salía de mi recámara, no podía ser una clínica, era **pos** un **recaladero,** un refugio elegante. Por aquella temporada estaba yo bajo la influencia de medicamentos, entienda usted, magistrado, así que mi memoria es vaga... poco después, me lo contaron, me informaron que estaba en Refugio Altar.

D: *When did you start walking again, Mr. García?*

R: A finales de febrero comencé a caminar dentro del centro, y por el patio del lugar. El sitio estaba cercado por un muro que no permitía la vista afuera y hacía imposible el escape.

D: *Did you have any exchange with anyone inside the shelter?*

R: Solo en camino al patio me topaba con guardias que protegían las salitas o dormitorios de mi zona. Estábamos divididos por zonas, pertenecía yo a la zona Zeta. No nos permitían mezclarnos. Nos vigilaban las veinticuatro horas del día, andábamos incomunicados, no permitían la más mínima conversación ni contacto entre los reos protegidos. Solo tenía yo contacto con el señor Moreno.

D: *Were you allowed visitors, Mr. García?*

R: Ni tan siquiera visitas. ¡Qué bien me hubiera hecho la visita de mi Lupe!

D: *Did they move you from Altar?*

R: Me reunía con el jefe de operativos de la policía local, el comandante Moreno, como les dije. Él era un señor de hablar sereno y que inspiraba confianza. A partir de ese momento sería mi contacto, me dijo. Él me entrevistaba en las tardes, y a él le suministraba información. El comandante Moreno me pidió que descansara en paz, que durmiera tranquilo, que me esperaban sesiones largas de entrevista, y que la protección estaba garantizada.

D: *So then what transpired after that, Mr. García López?*

R: Tres días después al comandante Moreno le rompieron el tórax.[31] Dicen que cenaba con su familia...

(D interrupts R.)

D: *Did you stay in town? Or did you move to another village or canton? Did you relocate to another state?*

---

[31] Sánchez, D. (16 de mayo, 2011). Balean sicarios a comandante de la Policía de Altar, Sonora. *Excelsior.* Recuperado de http://www.excelsior.com.mx/2011/05/16/nacional/737196

R: Pedí largarme del albergue, irme de Altar… bien lejos, bien lejos. **Luego luego** me dieron cobija en un refugio estatal. **Luego luego** me trasladaron a **Hermosío**, a un sitio conocido por La Mazmorra.

D: *Why did they agree to moving you out of that shelter?*

R: Les interesaba la información, mis contactos, mis historias.

D: *How long did you stay in La Mazmorra?*

R: Allí pernocté como por una semana. Ni respirar se podía en aquel demonio de lugar. Era un sitio seguro, pero de tránsito. Un lugar torturante, caluroso y maloliente. Después de tres semanas de martirio me volaron al D.F. Primera vez que montaba un avión, señor.

BLOCK 19. Federal shelter: Zócalo. Assault and escape.

D: *So, when exactly did they take you to Mexico City?*

R: Un día de asueto, se conmemoraba el natalicio del benemérito Juárez.

D: *And remind me again how much time elapsed since you started working for the judicial municipal police in Altar?*

R: Un año había pasado desde que comencé a colaborar con la policía.

D: *At that time, were you aware of the capture or indictment of any narco or suspected trafficker or even smugglers, Mr. García López?*

R: A muchos capos habían capturado, enjuiciado, incluso extraditado a los Estados Unidos.

D: *Because of your help?*

R: No sabría decirle. ¡Sabrá Dios!

D: *How was life in your new shelter, Mr. García?*

R: In Zócalo, Mr. Bollinger?

D: *CERTAINLY!*

R: Tenía mi propio apartamento… Los guardias entraban y salían armados, pero vestían de cuello y corbata… Era ambiente refinado, diferente… había otro tipo de gente, gente fina, muy formal… así era la atmósfera allí. La gente se saludaba y se despedía en español muy culto. No había olor ni a rancho ni a chancho, señores… En el edificio éramos unos quince, gente **grandota** y aunque no nos permitían mezclarnos, de noche los guardias relajaban las reglas. Pronto el grupo entró en confianza, después de darnos unos tequilas, y de cantarles yo mis corridos, entonces comenzaron a abrir el pico, y contar de historias de venganza, y sus anécdotas; eso sí, estaban todos muy preocupados con la protección dentro y fuera del refugio.

D: *But more or less, Mr. García, was life in Zócalo comfortable?*

R: No soportaba las comidas. Creía estar en una cárcel, porque ni salir nos permitían, a menos que solicitara uno un pase, y debía salir uno, muy bien acompañado. Solo un guardia de Monterey, el teniente Pena, me entendía bien, cuando yo le platicaba.

D: *Did you have any exchanges with other people who were protected in Zócalo?*

R: Ellos hacían anécdotas de sus hazañas y de historias de retaliación y venganza. Recomendaban protegerse al salir del edificio. Aquella no era vida, solo televisión, libros, leía los titulares de la prensa y ganas de vomitar me daba, solo se veían asesinatos y secuestros en la primera plana de cada periódico. Entonces teníamos las concebidas entrevistas que conducían oficiales tratando de recaudar información.

D: *Were you safe in Zócalo, Mr. García López?*

R: Creía yo estar a salvo.

D: *So, you weren't safe at all. You thought you were safe, but your life was in danger while you were under government protection.*

ACC: *Objection! That's not what the respondent said. Mr. Bollinger is leading the witness, Your Honor. He said he thought he was safe—*

IJ: *Sustained! Move on, Counselor.*

D: *Mr. García, please then tell this court what happened next—if anything.*

R: Lo peor ocurrió al mes de entrar en el que ya parecía un reclusorio. Resulta que El Potro, un **chavo** de unos veinte y tres o veintiún años, amaneció colgado del candelabro de su recámara. Fue aterrorizador porque El Potro era el hijastro de Candelario, alias El Chapa, un enanito, pero sanguinario jefe de una facción de los Zetas devenido en distribuidor de metanfetaminas, **perico**, **gallo** y **chiva**, así mismito como dice el corrido de Los Tucanes de Tijuana.

IJ: *Sir, just focus on the questions asked. Don't volunteer information. Remember the instructions at the beginning of the hearing?*

(R nods.)

D: *When did that incident occur, Mr. García?*

R: Un Jueves Santo.

IJ: *Could you be more specific—do you have a date?*

R: Un trece de abril... dos mil diecisiete, ¿el año? no recuerdo... Al mediodía encontraron al Potro.

D: *Did the guards do anything to protect the shelter moving forward?*

R: No lo creo. Después hubo una investigación, y los oficiales determinaron que había sido un suicidio.

BLOCK 20. Assault at Café La Rusa.

D: *Did you experience any other incident that made you feel unsafe in that federal safe house, and if so, when, Mr. García?*

R: Sí, sí, le platico… Muy cerca del Zócalo hay tiendas, hay sitios para cenar y beber, **pos** visitaba una de las cantinas de rutina, Café La Rusa, se llamaba o se llama, no sé. Había mozas bonitas, eso sí, las había polacas o rusas y chinitas. Iba a la cantina porque más que todo servían mi **Wakabaki** y otros platos sonorenses, bien picantones, los hacían. Pagaba a los guardias de turno por escaparme unas horas, y me iba a La Rusa. **Pos** una tarde me escapé al Café, y me cayó la noche ahí, tendrían que ser las cinco, y llovía, llovía muy duro. Yo tenía el presentimiento que no debía de estar allí, sobre todo de noche, era solo una corazonada. Estaba yo a punto de ser trasladado a otra casa refugio, y eso podría ocurrir en cualquier momento. El proceso estaba a punto de terminar y debía estar atento. Estando en la cantina, una de las mesas se ocupó por tres guardias encubiertos del Zócalo, ellos luciendo cachuchas rojas, señal que estaban activos, y era obvio que el protegido era el señor Bayardo, el cochino más gordo del corral. Los cuatro habían llegado ebrios como uvas... pagué y me salí corriendo a la calle… detrás de mí, sin más, estalló un tiroteo de **¡cate la boca!** El primero en caer fue el oficial Bayardo.[32]

D: *Who was officer Bayardo, Mr. García López?*

R: Un oficial de la policía federal quien dio la información que ayudó a encerrar a un montón de oficiales y a un alto jefe de la policía federal por corrupción y tráfico de estupefacientes, y conspiración en contrabando de armas.

BLOCK 21. Assault at Zócalo.

D: *So, were you afraid of any retaliation against your life, Mr. García?*

R: No tuve tiempo para temer, amanecí amarrado de pies a cabeza, y la cama mojada de petróleo.

D*: When?*

R: Domingo de Resurrección.

IJ: *Please, do we have a date, Mr. García?*

---

[32] Espino, M. (22 de julio, 2019). Testigos protegidos, en el abandono. *El Universal.* Recuperado de https://www.eluniversal.com.mx/nacion/seguridad/testigos-protegidos-programa-de-calderon-en-el-abandono

R: Dieciséis de abril… dos mil diecisiete. Y la fiesta estalló de madrugada.

D: *Obviously, they didn't burn you alive! So did they harm you in any way, Mr. García López?*

R: Mi cabeza no puede aguantar la memoria del castigo que recibí. Mientras dormía me cayeron encima varios hombres. Me taparon la cara con un trapo, ahí desperté... alguien me agarró por el cuello y muchos otros me patearon el estómago; **luego luego** me llenaron la boca con gaza, me golpearon con la cacha de una pistola o fusil, no recuerdo con qué, pero era como un metal pesado. Me dieron un **jodazo** en la cara que me durmió, no duré consciente un minuto. Amanecí con **choyacas**, moretones en las piernas, rasguños en los brazos, el cuerpo ensangrentado, el rostro desfigurado.

D: *Did the police give you any explanation of what happened?*

R: Me platicaron voces, trataron interrogarme, pero no recuerdo qué decían, ni si les dije algo, no tengo memorias de lo que pasó en la clínica. Cuando recuperé conciencia me dijeron que me habían dado más de veintiuna puñaladas en la espalda y que me habían perforado los pulmones y herido los riñones. Sé que me curaron en una clínica. Discúlpenme, fue en el Hospital de Jesús.

Tan pronto pude moverme, hui del Jesús.

D: *Where did you go, Mr. García?*

R: Regresé a Nogales, a mi Sonora.

BLOCK 22. Decision to leave Mexico. Entry to USA.
Flashback: lookout.

D: *Jesús, earlier you stated that you're terrified, that you didn't want to spend more time in government safe houses and that you decided to leave Mexico for good. Now, before coming to the United States, in what town did you live? Tell the court, please.*

R: Pernocté en varias casas en Nogales.

IJ: *In what state, sir?*

R: Sonora.

D: *Where in Nogales did you stay, Mr. García López?*

R: Escondido siempre… me quedé con ópatas, yaquis y mayos de los pueblos… estuve con conocidos míos, gente pobre, sabrá usted… Pernocté como le dije, en casas de compas, de gente que me quiso y respetó por el hombre que era yo. Regresé a comer mi **Wakabaqui**, mi **Gallina Pinta y Menudo**, mi **atole**, licenciado. Regresé a ver la danza del coyote y del venado. Les daba plata a mi gente eso sí, y ellos me mantenían como rey. Me

pude haber quedado allí para siempre, pero yo ya acostumbrado

a estar libre, a andar por la sierra, por el desierto y hasta por el

D.F... Yo era un halcón de desierto. Soy un hombre libre,

licenciado.

IJ: *Now, would you say that in Nogales there was heavy drug trafficking*

activity, Mr. García?

R: Oh sí, es un paso de cargas, hasta tiran la droga de un lado a

otro del muro que divide la frontera... los narcos usan bazukas

caseras para lanzar fardos de marihuana y si es necesario usan

catapultas medievales.

D: *So again, you were in danger, your life was at risk. Would you tell the*

court where you entered the United States, Mr. García López?

R: Por Altar, el desierto de Altar. Fui de Sonora a *Arizona*.

Crucé, yo solo crucé... y yo caminaba bajo una fuerte **resolana**,

así no hay quien te pille ni patrulle. ¡**A poco** se deshidrata uno!

Bien calientito que se pone el desierto señor.

D: *Rough terrain that you had to cross, Mr. García, right? Did you present*

yourself for inspection in any port of entry to come into Arizona,

Mr. García?

R: No entiendo su pregunta, licenciado. ¿Me explica intérprete?

IJ: *MR. GARCÍA, DID YOU ENTER LEGALLY OR ILLEGALLY INTO THE UNITED STATES?*

R: Con lo que yo sé, no necesito papeles, podría ser **pollero** o **coyote** señor.

D: *So, then explain how you actually, physically, were able to enter into the United States, Mr. García López.*

R: Caminé por el Altar, el desierto… La temperatura llega a los cien grados, facilito señor. El sol del desierto te hierve el pellejo, es bien calientico allá, y de noche te congelas el espinazo. Es un viaje insensato para el novicio. Cruzar el desierto es como cruzar los cráteres de la luna, dicen por ahí… Todo eso sin contar los bichos, insectos, las serpientes que te pican. Tenía dibujado el camino en mi cabeza. El camino, son de unas cuarenta a unas sesenta millas, en tres días, esto si sabes por dónde andas. Ojo con la serpiente cascabel, y así avanzas sin tropiezo. Hay puntos donde descansar, donde tomar agua, donde guarecerse, hay chozas, hay para hacer fuego de noche. Pero solo la experiencia te enseña. Al llegar a **Sasawk**, *Sasabe* como llaman los **yoris**, es un pasito a *Buenos Aires, Arizona*. Hay un trillo paralelo a la autopista 286, evitando siempre las garitas movibles que instalan los de la *Border Patrols*. Con suerte y en una de las guardarrayas te encuentras una bici o hasta una camioneta abandonada y le haces

por donde los traficantes van. Pero el tramo lo hice **a pincel**. Así

ocurrió, así llegué **al otro lado**.

D: *Why did you cross through the Altar Desert, Mr. García López?*

R: Manejé una **charanga** que compré en un **corralón** municipal

en Nogales, por solo ocho mil pesos saqué un *Chevrolet Fleetmaster*

del cuarenta o cincuenta, y manejé hasta el mero desierto;

conocía el desierto Altar como la palma de mis manos. Esa es la

razón.

D: *Tell us about the circumstances that made you know the Altar Desert.*

In other words, how and why did you become familiar with the Altar

Desert, Mr. García López?

R: Yo fui **halcón** en Altar y en otros cerros de la frontera con **el**

otro lado. Pero cuando me enteré que comenzaron a capturar

halcones y llevárselos directico a la Fiscalía de *Arizona*, en vez

de meterse en el país, como un emigrante más, como hacían

muchos **chavos**, me regresé a Sonora. Fue entonces que

apareció la **chamba** de abrir hoyos y así empecé en el artilugio

de los túneles.

D: *Why were they jailing lookouts, Mr. García?*

R: Cuando vieron que los **punteros** tenían equipos bravos, herramientas que usan los meros militares, radios de frecuencia secreta, entonces se les tiraron encima y los apresaron. ¡Y no te devolvían a México!

D: *What did you do working as a lookout, Mr. García López?*

R: Vigilar los movimientos de la patrulla fronteriza más que nada.

IJ: *Did you know what type of trafficking was being carried out through the desert—Altar Desert, for instance—Mr. García?*

R: ¿Qué no pasó por el desierto, licenciado? bolsitas de *fentanyl*, cánnabis, metanfetamina, heroína, cocaína, hombres, mujeres y niños, la madre de los tomates.

BLOCK 23. Narco-style. Narco-corrido. Mariachis.

D: *Your Honor, I would like to call your attention to Exhibit 22. There's a picture of what seems to be a mariachi band. Do you recognize yourself in the picture, Mr. García López?*

R: Sí, ese soy, y mi guitarra, licenciado.

D: *Can you identify that group of musicians, Mr. García López?*

R: ¡**Añil**! Son Los Halcones del Cerro.

D: *What connection, if any, did you have with Los Halcones del Cerro, Mr. García López?*

R: Yo fui el mánager de la banda, más bien yo les representé, fui por un tiempo el gerente de Los Halcones del Cerro.

D: *So, at some point, did you switch to the music business, Mr. García López?*

R: Nooo… ¿cómo le explico? Me gusta el mariachi, compongo corridos. En una época organicé **baile de monte**, licenciado. Ya que conocía a gente de plata, les hice fiestas, sobre todo a buchones, a honchos, a quienes se le sirve la música en reuniones o en peleas de gallos, incluso para bodas y quinceañeras. Se hacía buena plata, licenciado.

D: *So, you also delved into the managing of music groups, Mr. García?*

R: Muchos sujetos me preguntaban si yo conocía una banda de mariachis para **guarachar**, para sus fiestas, y yo les conseguía a los muchachos. **¡Cate monte ilichi!** Y mucha plata que hice, licenciado.

D: *How did you come in contact with Los Halcones del Cerro, Mr. García López?*

R: Bueno, yo pasaba por el Parque Emiliana de Zubeldía Inda, muy a menudo, y veía a unos mocosos haciendo de mariachis.

Siempre les tiraba una **lanita** para que hicieran sus cosas y se

compraran su **churro** ¿por qué no? Eran unos pobres **chavos**,

uno de ellos que era **yaqui**, pues él mendigaba y se las pasaba

diciendo, "**Cahita tomi**". Que eso quiere decir, no hay plata.

Pero a pesar de su pobreza, los mocosos tocaban mejor…

sonaban mejor… que las bandas de supuestos profesionales con

los que me relacionaba y a los que contrataba. Yo lidiaba con

viejos bien babosos y desafinados, al lado de los mocosos

mendigos, señores y señoras. **Pos**, les dije a los mocosos, así les

puse, vea usted: Los Mocosos del Parque, ese fue su primer

apodo que les puse. Entonces les pregunté que si querían tocar

para mí, y que a cambio me tenían que componer un corrido a

mi nombre, y así fue que lo hicieron.

D: *Did you sing those lyrics as part of the shows you had here in Yuma,*
Mr. García?

R: Añil, licenciado.

D: *Mr. García, were those lyrics offensive or would anyone think you are a*
narco because of it?

R: Nel, licenciado, de ningún modo señor. Es un corrido

padrazo, suena a narco-corrido, pero no no lo es, es solo un

corrido y nada más. Ese es uno de los mejorcitos que entono, y a cada fiesta que iban Los Mocosos del Parque, bueno depués

Los Halcones del Cerro, les solicitaban el corridito. A los **chavos**

también le llamaban, La Banda del Güero García. Así le apodó el

público, en honor a mi persona, pero yo los terminé llamando,

Los Halcones del Cerro, así los bauticé profesionalmente.

D: *Do you know the lyrics of the narco-corrido they composed in your name,*

Mr. García López?

R: Pos, claro que sí, como les dije es un padrazo corrido.

Ahorita, no recuerdo la letra porque estoy de puro nervios,

licenciado. Pero aquellos fueron buenos momentos, yo me

divertía en las fiestas con mi mariachi, y sus corridos y se hizo

mucha plata.

D: *Did you make good money in the clubs here in Yuma, Mr. García?*

R: Meros pesitos de propina, licenciado que humildemente

alcanza para el pan y la gasolina.

D: *What ever happened to La Banda del Güero, or as you baptized them*

later on, Los Halcones del Cerro, Mr. García López?

R: Los chicos desaparecieron de la tierra. No sé qué pasó con

mis mariachis.

IJ: *So, would it be fair to say that you were known in the community as someone connected to drug kingpins and narcotrafficking, Mr. García López?*

R: Pos sí, mire usted era una doble vida. Yo hice mucha **lana** con la construcción. Yo levanté un imperio con mis manos, licenciado. **Ahorita**, yo no sé qué pensó la gente de mí, pero yo sí vestía bien **fachoso**, como le platiqué ya. Me gustaba calzar botas con punteras de piel de mula, mis **trocas** pintadas **con llaves** en el **bumperdefensa**. Me encantan mis camisonas de ceda. Mis correas tenían sus hebillas gordas de oro, señoras y señores. ¡Y era todo! Pero creo que mis trocas hablaban de un hombre trabajador, un hombre de negocios. Nadie pudo identificarme como narco, si no como constructor, a pesar de que mis asociados eran los narcos.

D: *Mr. García López, you said that your trucks bore the name* **Constructora Querobabi**, *right?*

R: Añil. Así, así es, licenciado.

D: *So, no one could say that you were a narcotrafficker or had any affiliation with smuggling drugs, drug paraphernalia or anything of the sort, right, Mr. García?*

R: Bueno, yo era **fachoso**, licenciado, no era cocinero.

D: *Mr. García, you even stated in your affidavit that the municipal police thought you were connected to the cartels. Can you explain?*

R: No sé, no sé, entre soplones y envidiosos... ¿qué se va a esperar? Hay muchos soplones, hay muchos impostores, y no falta la gente celosa, los hay resentidos también. Hay gente que se la pasa en el **chismarajo**, sin mucho que hacer, su señoría. ¿Usted ve? Y habla que te habla y chismosea. Y claro, me relacionaba con gente grandota, con buchones, y les construía, les servía...

(D interrupts R.)

D: *Were you a drug smuggler, Jesus?*

R: *Hell no!*

D: *Jesús, no one thought you were a policeman, nor did you ever dress as one, right?*

R: **¡Ehui!** Así es, licenciado.

D: *I have no further questions, Your Honor.*

End of direct examination by respondent's attorney,

Mr. Bollinger.

Lunch break.

**Commencement of cross-examination by the ACC,
Ms. López**

**BLOCK 1. Cross. Verify which authority apprehends
Mr. García López.**

ACC: *Mr. García López, did anyone help you fill out this application, the
Form I-589?*

R: ¡**Añil**, señora! En el bufete del licenciado *Bollinger*, en
Hermosillo, aquí mismito en *Yuma* como le platiqué
anteriormente.

ACC: *So, that application was filled out after you were in ICE custody,
Mr. García López. Would that be fair to say, Mr. García?*

*(R stares at ACC, then looks up to the ceiling and moves his hands in the
direction of his counsel.)*

IJ: *Sir?*

R: *Yes sir!*

ACC: *Mr. García, explain to this court why you ended up in ICE custody
to begin with?*

R: Pos sí... saliendo del *Yuma International Airport*, allá por la
South Pacific Avenue con *Gila Ridge Road*, una patrulla detuvo el
vehículo que iba yo manejando... Los **cuicos** me pidieron,

decentemente eso sí, que saliera del vehículo… me pidieron

identificación… no llevaba identificación encima... **ahorita** y si

no mal recuerdo, me pidieron licencia de conducción, registro y

seguranza, la póliza... A mi amigo, también, le pidieron que se

bajara de la **charanga**… Creo que revisaron el vehículo...

después se largaron a **checar** algo en sus monitores, **recalaron** y

fue cuando nos pidieron que les acompañaran a los ellos. A mí

me llevaron a una oficina... allí me interrogaron…

(ACC interrupts R.)

ACC: *Was it regular local police or an ICE officer that took you into*

custody, sir?

R: Los **cuicos** me llevaron, señorita.

ACC: *What were the circumstances of your arrest, Mr. García?*

R: No le entendí la pregunta a la señorita agente… ¿me repite

intérprete?

ACC: *How come you ended up arrested, Mr. García?*

R: En la *Superior Court, in Yuma county.* Allí me asignaron un

defensor público, *Mr. Hayes,* creo que así se llama, un moreno él,

alto y de patillas grandes y bigotón de mariachi… *Mr. Hayes* me

dijo que había una investigación por hurto y homicidio a balazos

a un policía encubierto. Alguien, no sé quién, hizo una llamada a la estación de policías... no sé de quién se trataba, pero alguien hizo una llamada anónima... se dice que una voz joven llamó, una *teenager* llamó a la estación policial... *The teen,* la voz, se comunicó con la policía para colectar un rescate que pagaban, eran unos quince mil quinientos o diecisiete mil dólares, un botín grandote. El abogado me dijo que la **chirinolera,** era una desconocida que llamó a la **cuicada,** y la voz dio mis señas, y dio la descripción del *RV* y la placa numerada de mi **charanga.** ¡Pura coincidencia! Y así **a trochis mochis, a mata caballo,** me arrestaron, señorita.

ACC: *Were you drunk at the time of your arrest?*

R: ¿Cómo así?

ACC: *Were you impaired while conducting your RV?*

R: ¿Impedido? *When?*

ACC: *Were you under the influence of any narcotics, any drugs or alcohol, at the time of your arrest?*

R: No sabría qué decirle, señora agente. ¿Señorita intérprete me puede explicar?

IJ: *SIR, STOP! STOP TALKING AND LISTEN TO THE QUESTION, PLEASE!*

ACC: *Thank you, Your Honor, but I'll rephrase my question for the respondent. Sir, the police conducted a field sobriety test, and the breathalyzer marked point fifteen percent (0.15 percent) of BAC, way above the minimum of point zero eight percent (0.08 percent).*

R: *Who? Me? Are you talking to me?*

ACC: *Yes, sir, you! Sir, sir, do you think you have alcohol or drug dependency? In order words, are you an alcoholic or an addict, sir?*

R: ¿Drogadicto? Nooo, no señorita, de ningún modo.

ACC: *Were you injured when manacles were put on you, Mr. García?*

R: No sé qué me pregunta.

(R stares around at everyone in the courtroom.)

ACC: *Let me backtrack—were you driving erratically, swerving in and out of lanes while driving on South Pacific Avenue after leaving the airport, and that's when you were stopped?*

R: *I was fastening my seat belt.*

(R pauses. IJ interrupts R's silence.)

IJ: ¡En español, Jesús! Su testimonio debe ser en español. ¡No más inglés, por favor!

R: *Sorry!*

IJ: *Mr. García you confirmed this morning at the commencement of your asylum hearing that the language that you best speak and understand is*

Spanish, so speak Spanish Mr. García, and wait for the interpreter to interpret!

ACC: *Sir, were you consuming drugs while living in Mexico?*

R: No, ¿cómo le platico sobre el caso? No todo el tiempo, no.

ACC: *When did you begin taking drugs, then?*

R: A poco, después de ir a la Judicial, **pos** no podía dormir.

ACC: *Mr. García, were you the one who committed the homicide and theft of which you've been accused?*

(D abruptly stands and raises his right hand.)

D: *OBJECTION, YOUR HONOR, OBJECTION—*

(IJ interrupts D.)

IJ: *What's your objection, Mr. Bollinger?*

D: *It is true that there's an investigation pending, but Jesús Antonio García López maintains his innocence. If anything, he sustains that the only crime he committed was the purchase of a stolen recreational vehicle without knowing that the vehicle had been stolen. The RV in question drew the attention of the patrol police because of the pictures of marijuana leaves and slogans with pictures of adolescents who seemed to be smoking grass, but Mr. García López had just purchased the van and was in the process of removing those pictures. I object also in that this question asks Mr. García López to waive his Fifth Amendment right to self-incrimination.*

IJ: *Sustained! Move on, Madam Counsel—*

(ACC pauses.)

ACC: *I'll rephrase the question for you, Mr. García: Wouldn't you agree that the night you were stopped by the police, you had a few drinks in you?*

R: *Yes, only a few.* Unos **meros pistos**.

ACC: *Mr. García López, were you involved in the robbery and death of which you've been accused in the Superior Court in Yuma County?*

D: *Objection!*

IJ: *Sustained!*

R: ¡Nel!

ACC: *Let's move on to another set of questions, sir.*

BLOCK 2. Cross. Liaison between cartels and the police.

ACC: *Mr. García López, you mentioned during direct examination by Mr. Bollinger that you performed a number of jobs for the cartels, your associates. What exactly did you do for the cartels?*

R: Puro negocios, puro *business*, señorita. Yo conocía a mucha gente, y a cada quien y de vez en vez le hacía un favor. Más adelante fui la conexión entre la policía y los jefes, los pejes gordos, señorita. Por ejemplo, llamaba y ponía anuncios en los periódicos, daba dádivas a la **chorcha**, les hacía favores a diputados, a gente de la alcaldía. Era el enlace entre negociantes y muchas instituciones.

ACC: *Mr. García, what bosses are you referring by the* pejes gordos?

R: Puros hombres de negocio, señorita. Me relacionaba con el Gaviota, el Chavito, los Güeros. Para muchos de ellos trabajé.

(ACC puts on her glasses and reads from a piece of paper on her desk.)

ACC: *Mr. García, could you elaborate on the fact that you were the liaison between the newspapers, several institutions, your associates, the cartels and the police?*

R: Se hacía ofrendas a iglesias, como ya dije… yo a veces… llevaba diezmos a **chorchas**… eran especie de dádivas y donativos que se hacían a sacerdotes populares de comunidades donde mis asociados tenían intereses. Yo personalmente mandé a construir capillas, conventos, mausoleos y escuelas. Hablando de construcción, **pos** construí canchas de fútbol, canchas de *baseball*, siempre a nombre de una u otra organización, en dependencia de quien aportaba la **lana**.

ACC: *Mr. García, here is my question, and I'll repeat it: Were you the liaison between the newspapers and your associates and what exactly did you do?*

R: El agente PZ me dio el visto bueno para colaborar en todo lo posible con mis asociados, y uno de los trabajos fue llamar a la prensa, y, y, y informar de **levantones**, de ataques, de secuestros en los que grupúsculos enemigos se iban a involucrar, señorita. La prensa tenía que reportar lo que los jefes mandaban ¿me entiende **ahorita**?

ACC: *Thank you, Mr. García. Okay, I understand that. What other transactions or businesses did you delve into that involved your associates and any other institutions? Can you think of anything else?*

R: Puedo explicarle, me gustan los animales, me gustan los **machos** en particular. Entonces vi la **chanza** de entrar en la compra y venta de **Caballos de Cuarto de Milla, de Generosos** y ganado vacuno y bovino. Compraba las bestias para mis asociados, señorita; especialmente me gustaban los caballos azabaches y zainos. Después de las **corridas**, donde se herraban las crías y les hacían **señales de sangre**, era yo quien coordinaba la entrega de las bestias, para después ser vendidas y exportadas a compradores en *Yuma* y otras ciudades **del otro lado**.

ACC: *Did you have a ranch or stable or barns for the cattle you dealt in, Mr. García?*

R: Nel, pero me gustan los caballos, sobre todo los **retintos** de Arabia, como menta el corrido 'El Profeta'. Les cuento, a los establos de **Hermosío**, me llegaron muchos potrillos de los más finos, y de ahí se iban rapidito para San Diego, para *Yuma* y adónde Dios pidiera, señorita... Yo velaba, yo inspeccionaba los establos, era mi pasión, señorita... y tenía mozas de cuadras que limpiaban los establos a menudo... Era yo quien mantenía las bestias casi de semanita a semanita, señorita, y de la mano se me iban **pos**, se vendían requerapidito... Cuidaba a mis bestias como se cuida al oro y la plata, señorita.

ACC: *Did you use your true identity to effectuate some of the purchases?*

R: Depende, señorita... a veces sí otras no... depende de la época, depende de la misión. ¿No cree usted?

ACC: *So then, were you a straw buyer and seller, Mr. García, for those transactions?*

R: No, yo no fui ni espantapájaros ni fantasma. Yo solo inspeccionaba el animal, lo compraba y vendía... así ganaba mucha **lana**.

ACC: *Well, if all you did was lend your legal name to complete all those sales and purchases, then you were a figurehead, a middleman, weren't you, Mr. García?*

R: No sé lo que es testaferro, pero como le expliqué, mi gente, mis asociados, ellos estaban ocupados, y yo compraba y vendía las bestias. Era mi tarea preferida ir personalmente los domingos en la mañana. **Ay nomás**.

ACC: *Did you finish?*

R: ¡Aha!

ACC: *How big were those transactions on Sunday mornings, sir?*

R: ¿Al mes?

ACC: *Okay, monthly?*

R: De un millón a a a dos milloncitos y medio, señorita.

ACC: Pesos *or dollars?*

R: Dólares, señorita… dólares, sí… Aquí se juega al duro y sin guante.

ACC: *So, in essence you did some serious business for the narcos, more than just PR. Isn't that right, Mr. García?*

R: *PR?*

ACC: *Yes!*

(ACC is writing on a pad while asking questions.)

ACC: *PR, sir, public relations. Didn't you?*

R: Puro negocios, señorita.

ACC: *Isn't it true that you kept a ledger, Mr. García?*

R: El original se lo entregué al agente PZ.

ACC: *I don't believe you didn't have more than one ledger, Mr. García, taking into account the vast array of business you managed. Did you keep any accounting? Other than the ledger you said you handed over to agent PZ, didn't you create a new set of books, sir?*

R: Sí, creé muchos libros, todo lo anotaba y guardaba, y los entregué a los Federales.

ACC: *Would it be fair to say that you were the logistic lieutenant of the Grupo Operativo del Pacífico Ltd, for which Gaviota and Chavito were the main lieutenants?*

R: Yo no tengo título de nada, si acaso mi único título es El Güero García. Yo soy hombre de negocios, señores... Mire usted, a mí me llamaban de todas partes. A mí me pedían que hiciera tal y más cuál cosa, y yo por la plata corría a resolver el problema. Y tenía bien presente que tenía que dar información a mis protectores. Era más simple que simplón, señorita...

(R pauses and stares at ACC.)

R: La pobreza es fea, señorita. Esa era mi cruz. Entonces aprendí que mi única salida era hacer negocios y vivir bien. Después se pusieron las cosas **pinche** feas y tuve que trabajar para la Municipal y para los narcos. No fue mi culpa. A mí me metieron en el hoyo.

ACC: *Were you involved in the sale of illegal drugs or narcotics?*

R: ¡No señor!

BLOCK 3. Cross. Narco-corrido.

ACC: *Your Honor, in Exhibit 32, Tab OO, on page 112, you can see the lyrics of a* corrido *for which the title is* "El Güero García," *and there are just a few stanzas.*

IJ: *HAS THE* CORRIDO *BEEN TRANSLATED, MS. LÓPEZ?*

ACC: *No, unfortunately, it has not—but, Your Honor, with your indulgence and the assistance of the interpreter, I'd like to have it read and moved into evidence. These lyrics were found on the Internet. I transcribed some of the stanzas. Can we use the services of the interpreter for the purpose of translating some of the stanzas?*

IJ: *Do you need a minute to go through it, Madam Interpreter? Please read the Spanish version out loud and then sight-translate it.*

(The interpreter silently reads the lyrics.)

El Güero García.

(Shrieking): Válgame Dios ahí va El Güero **embuchonado**.

(Soloist): Ahí va Jesusito El Güero empedernido que exhibe gorro fino y calibres en sus manos.

(Chorus): Ahí va Jesusito El Güero empedernido.

(Soloist): Ahí va Jesusito El Güero **ajoliscado** *que temen en presencia de troca y cuerno de chivo.*

(Chorus): Ahí va Jesusito El Güero **ajoliscado**.

(Soloist): Jesusito no dispara, pero mata. No confundas su tamaño que te ataca.

Ahí va Jesusito con **morras** *en su* **troca**, *con oro que rechina y* **bramona** *de sus vacas.*

ACC: *Did you in fact compose those lyrics, Mr. García?*

R: Yo compongo sí, pero esos que recitó la señorita, esos no son de mi autoría. Son buenos corridos, ¿verdad? **Pos**, desgraciadamente no los compuse yo.

ACC: *You'll probably agree with me that those lyrics depict the life of a narco, Mr. García? Do you agree?*

R: Está equivocada, señorita. Ese es el estilo de un ranchero con sus mujeres y su ganado, con su **picapón** y sus armas y respeto que se merece. Se equivoca, señorita… disculpe, pero se equivocó, señorita.

BLOCK 4. Cross. Civilian vs. policeman. Police uniforms.

ACC: *Mr. García, you earlier testified that because your trucks bore the name* Constructora Querobabi, *no one could have recognized you as a narcotrafficker, right?*

R: Añil, señora. Segurito.

ACC: *But yet, Mr. García, you even stated in your affidavit of support for your own I-589 application that the municipal police force thought you were connected to the cartels! Were you in fact in cahoots with the cartels, Mr. García? This is before the police made you an informant.*

R: ¡No señorita no! ¿Pero mira que hay gente envidiosa? Hay muchos soplones por ahí, gente envidiosa. Son gentuza que por hablar entierra a su madre.

ACC: *Mr. García, isn't it true that you admitted during direct examination that you worked with narcos and drug traffickers, whether you knew their line of work or not?*

R: ¡Es cierto!

ACC: *On the other hand, Mr. García, no one thought of you as a policeman and no one ever saw you dressed as one, right, Mr. García?*

R: Así es, agente. **Añil**, licenciados.

ACC: *I am going to show the witness Exhibit 33. In this exhibit, there are several pictures where Mr. García is dressed in military fatigues, in a T-*

shirt with the police force logo, half-wearing a balaclava, and there are eight

pictures in total where the respondent is wearing various military garments.

(The bailiff hands pictures to R.)

ACC: *Sir, do you recognize the pictures the bailiff is handing to you? And is that you in every picture I've shown to you?*

R: Edá ¡Sí señorita!

(R smiles and shuffles through the pictures.)

ACC: *Sir, is it possible that you dressed as a policeman because, in fact, you worked for the force as a policeman?*

R: Simplemente vestía con las ropas de **chota** como camuflaje, señorita.

ACC: *What do you mean by wearing it as a disguise, Mr. García?*

R: Como tapujo, disimulo, mero enmascaramiento, cosa que si alguien me vio cuando probaba mis armas no se atrevía a meterse conmigo.

ACC: *So, in spite of multiple pictures of you dressed as a member of the police force and as an army officer, it is your statement that you didn't work for the Mexican law enforcement authorities in any capacity?*

R: Como militar… ¿cómo militar? No, nunca trabajé como militar. La respuesta es no, no, no, nunca… se lo aseguro, señorita.

ACC: *Dressed in a turtleneck, in the desert, Mr. García? Hard to believe.*
Did you ever dress up in police uniforms in front of civilians? In other words,
did you ever impersonate a cop or a member of the army while living in
Mexico or any other part of the world, sir?

R: ¡Nel!

ACC: *So, you never brandished a police insignia or ever showed a police*
badge to a civilian, sir?

R: ¿De la **chota**? ¡Nunca!

ACC: *Did you ever have Zetas member or Knight Templars Cartel*
member decals on any of your vehicles to carry out any criminal operations
against the civilian population, as those criminal organizations often do, sir?

R: No señorita, ya le platiqué, señorita. La única intención fue de
ir al cerro a disparar. Mucha gente lo hace, se disfraza, simula,
pretende solo por hacer puro fuego.

ACC: *Okay, Mr. García! Did you ever carry out any criminal operation*
against civilians?

R: *No, never!*

ACC: *Never dressed like an AFI agent to release anyone from prison?*
(The interpreter asks for clarification.)

ACC: *AFI, the Federal Investigation Agency, Madam Interpreter.*

R: ¡No señor!

BLOCK 5. Cross. Security guard. Recruitment.

ACC: *Sir, you stated earlier that you provided, in fact* sold, *police uniforms to different individuals. Did you acquire those uniforms while working as a security guard?*

D: *OBJECTION, YOUR HONOR. FOUNDATION?*

IJ: *Overruled!*

ACC: *Your Honor, our records show that Mr. Jesús Antonio García López worked as a security guard from September to December 2011. Did you or did you not work as a guard for the mines, Mr. García?*

R: ¡Nooo! No, señorita, yo... ¿me puede repetir la pregunta por favor? *Please!*

ACC: *Did you work as a security guard from approximately September to the end of the year 2011 or didn't you, Mr. García?*

R: Las fechas no recuerdo, pero sí recuerdo que **chambeé** como *security guard.*

ACC: *Did you also recruit security guards for some of your associates, Mr. García?*

D: *Objection, Your Honor. Foundation again!*

IJ: *Overruled! Move on please.*

ACC: *Your Honor, we have information from two of the three mining companies that the respondent, Mr. García, worked for. In addition, the* *information says that Mr. Pantaleón García returned years later to those companies and was asking security guard personnel to join his own security firm. My question to you, Mr. García, is: Were you trying to recruit individuals for an alleged security firm of yours or not?*

D: *Objection, Your Honor. His name is not Pantaleón.*

IJ: *Sir, did you ever use the name Pantaleón for any business enterprise or to procure employment in the mines?*

R: ¡No! Pantaleón era uno de los sobrinos de un capataz. Ya se lo platiqué. ¡No me confundan! Como le platiqué, puede que me hayan confundido con Pantaleón, pero yo nunca usé un nombre tan ridículo como ese. ¡No!

IJ: *Proceed, Ms. López!*

ACC: *So, my question to you again, Mr. García, is: Were you trying to recruit individuals for an alleged security firm of yours or not?*

R: No supe yo que los guardas terminarían trabajando para cárteles, señorita.

ACC: *That wasn't my question, sir, but thank you.*

R: ¿Perdón?

ACC: *So, let me ask you: Why were you scouting for trained security guards all over the place, Mr. García?*

D: *Objection! Mr. García only went to two job sites.*

IJ: *I'll allow it. Answer the question, Mr. García!*

R: *Question?*

ACC: *Thank you, Your Honor. Let me repeat the question. Why were you scouting for trained security guards in the mines, Mr. García?*

R: Algunos asociados me pidieron guardias entrenados y con experiencia para cuidar de sus **cantones**, almacenes y negocios. Los mineros preparaban bien a sus guardias. Esa gente sabía muy bien cómo cargar-descargar armas, limpiar cañones, escoger armas para las tareas, era gente preparada para tirar. Los guardias hacen prácticas de tiro al blanco con todo tipo de armas de la armería. Las minas tenían buenos tiradores, gente lista para la acción, gente joven, hábil y dispuesta, no eran gordos babosos, magistrado. Además, la paga les iba a venir requetebién, era buena **lana**.

BLOCK 6. Cross. Beginnings as an informant.

ACC: *And, Mr. García López, isn't it true that because of all the information you knew and all the experience you had in business and dealing with the people you dealt with, you were a valuable man to the municipal police force and later on to the Mexican Federal Police?*

R: Así es, señorita.

ACC: *When did you become an informant, Mr. García López?*

R: De joven.

ACC: *My question is when* exactly *did you become one?*

R: Nomás que las circunstancias apretaron, señorita… tuve que ser muy inteligente para sobrevivir, agente.

(R lowers his head and stops talking.)

ACC: *When did you become an informant for the first time, Mr. García?*

R: Así gané la vida de **vuqui**, señorita. Para sobrevivir tuve que trabajar duro. A veces la vida no te ofrece otra opción.

ACC: *Could you explain what you mean by that, Mr. García?*

R: Añil, agente. **Pos**, un buen día, un señor importante se me acercó, algo **tiriciento** él… **pos**, me agarró por el **pescuezo** y me gritó, "¿**güerito**, para quién trabajas?". Sepa usted que en el pueblo se usaban a los **plebes** para informar, vigilar y hasta espiar matrimonios… entonces con mucho miedo le respondí: "**Chambeo** para Puñal, señor".

ACC: *Sir, who is Puñal?*

IJ: *Interpreter, what's the meaning of Puñal and could you spell it for the record, please?*

R: Puñal era un encarnecido sicario… No recuerdo exactamente cuándo, pero tendría yo unos dieciocho o diecinueve años, y mi padre, el señor García, me encomendó al señor Cortéz.

Entonces el viejo Cortéz, este, este… me llevó a San Luis Río Colorado, al cultivo de flores.

ACC: *Where is San Luis Río Colorado, Mr. García?*

R: En Sonora, estamos hablando de la frontera con *Arizona*, a pocas millas de *Yuma*. Allí conocí a Puñal. No pasó una semana de haber llegado al campo y los hombres del sicario me raptaron. Puñal se aseguró de que me alimentaran y me dio un poco de **lana** a cambio de información.

(ACC uses R's pause to question him.)

ACC: *Why was Puñal feeding you and giving you money? I don't comprehend——*

(ACC gestures in a puzzled manner and R answers.)

R: Para informar, señorita… información buscaba el hombrín… Me dijo, "**Échame agua güerito**", espía y avísame cuando los grandotes muevan su carga.

(ACC uses R's pause to question him.)

ACC: *¿Informar? To inform about what, Mr. López García?*

R: Pos, había familias de grandes negocios en la Ciudad, los García, los Hernández, los Jimenez, cada quien, con ganado, carreras de caballos, siembras, camiones, maquiladoras; pero ellos almacenaban, empacaban y movían mercancía.

(R signals with his hand the idea of quote, unquote.)

R: "Carga." Hasta la policía estaba involucrada en el **desmadre**.

ACC: *How did you get that information, Mr. García?*

R: Yo escuché del mismísimo Puñal.

ACC: *How were you supposed to get the information about the drug shipments?*

R: Trabajaba yo para los Hernandez y en poco tiempo me gané la confianza de los capataces. Yo escuchaba más de la cuenta.

ACC: *So, what happened?*

R: Apareció el señor Porfirio Dámaso a quien de estúpido le confesé que los hombres de Puñal me habían dado una golpiza y secuestrado.

ACC: *Wait, wait, who is Porfirio Dámaso?*

R: El médico que me atendió.

ACC: *What did the doctor do to you? Did you say that it was a bad move telling him about Puñal?*

R: Porfirio quiso entrar en el juego y **nomás** me ofreció **feria** para que le informara cuando Puñal movía su carga, en qué transporte la movía, a qué hora, nombres de los encargados, y para dónde iban los cargamentos.

ACC: *How much money did Porfirio offer you?*

R: No más **feria**, señorita. Unos meros pesitos, muy poco… casi nada… decía él que estaba creando su imperio… pero de que se enriqueció se enriqueció, eso sí, con mi información robó cargamentos, hizo su **desmadre** también.

ACC: *How much money exactly did you receive?*

R: Me daba cien pesitos por movida, no más; el hombre venía y me dejaba caer la **lana** a los días de yo darle información… **Luego luego** la situación cambió, y en una ocasión me chantajeó, no quiso darme más plata, solo protección, pues había mucha matanza, por todas las calles había muertos.

IJ: *Sir, I'm confused. Who was that "hombre?" Do you have a name for that man, sir?*

R: Porfirio, Porfirio Dámaso, él está aquí en *Yuma*, aquí lo vi, por las calles… Porfirio escapó cuando se dieron cuenta que era un charlatán… un líder de rateros que se hacía pasar por vigilante.

IJ: *Okay, once again I'm confused, Mr. García. Could you tell us who Mr. Porfirio Dámaso is? I mean the whole story, not just in bits and pieces, please?*

R: Se decía en las calles que Porfirio era médico de chivas, un veterinario que mató más vacas de las que curó. Porfirio hacía de médico comunitario y después se metió de líder contra las pandillas y narcos. Era un agitador. Para proteger la comunidad se valía de tres grupos comunitarios: Las Sombras, Comités de Defensa, y los Antinarcos. Los tres grupos terminaron robando, asaltando y extorsionando a la población, incluso cobraban derecho de piso a comerciantes... **Luego luego** la Federal llegó al pueblo y convirtió a algunos de los hombres en parte de su fuerza de vigilancia, de los Federales, quiero decir... el resto siguió en su relajo con Porfirio. **Pos**, Porfirio armó mucho lío después que los hacendados se dieron cuenta de que él quiso proclamarse el Simón Bolívar del pueblo, El Libertador de los Humildes, hasta se hizo llamar. Porfirio en su condición de libertador ponía anuncios en periódicos y llamaba a las comunidades a organizarse y pelear. El muy sinvergüenza, hasta se hizo de un programa de radio llamando a los pobladores que se armaran y le dieran plata a él, esto ocurrió después de formar las tres bandas que les platiqué... Como les platicaba, el **carajada** pedía a la comunidad que se agrupara en brigadas contra los hombres de negocio, a los que les llamaba narcos. Por una parte, tenía razón, por otra, aquello olía a oportunismo. El doctorcito era pura fachada. Yo tuve suerte, mucha suerte, y escapé a cerro Carnero antes de que me aniquilara.

IJ: *Why and how did you escape, sir? You were under the tutelage of Puñal, also watched and working for Porfirio and working for the powerful narcos* hacendados, *even making money in the process.*

R: No tuve otra, magistrado.

ACC: *How did you escape, Mr. García?*

(R laughs.)

R: Buena pregunta, señorita, muy buena pregunta. **Pos**, Porfirio Dámaso mentó mi nombre en una comparecencia radial. Entonces su enfermera y amante del señor licenciado, La Gorda le llamaban… **pos**, La Gorda me dijo, "huye Carita, huye". Carita me llamaba ella con mucho cariño. **Pos**, La Gorda, insistió, "Tú no caigas preso, vas a perder tu integridad". Yo sabía que me violarían si caía en un penal, por eso hui. La Gorda me ayudó.

BLOCK 7. Cross. ICE. Detention in Yuma, Arizona.

ACC: *Let's go back for a second to September 13 of this year when you were apprehended in Yuma—*

(R interrupts ACC.)

R: La chota, la chota, sí, ella dio conmigo… ya le dije antes, agente.

ACC: *You mean the police, Mr. García? Right?*

R: La policía y la migra son la misma **pinche** fuerza, licenciada.

ACC: *I am not going to comment on that statement, Mr. García. Now where and how did that arrest happen, Mr. García?*

R: La vida da muchas vueltas, señorita. Les dije que estuve cantando en un antro, como por unos tres meses…

(ACC interrupts R.)

ACC: *Who did you sing for, sir?*

R: Cantaba con Los Hijos de Negrete, una banda de mariachi local.

(R stops his testimony and stares at ACC.)

ACC: *PROCEED, SIR!*

R: Mi vida andaba bien, sin tropiezos ni inconvenientes, hasta que una noche pedí las llaves de la **troca** al trompeta de la banda, en el único que podía confiar. El trompeta me dio las llaves porque pensó que iba por **morras** y regresaría; pero yo **andaba pedo** y me descarrilé por una cuneta. Fue cuando la **chota** me encontró con la **charanga** puesta de sombrero. El policía me salvó la vida cuando la **troca** estaba a punto de estallar. Y yo dormido ni me enteré. Me pude haber achicharrado, licenciados. ¿Se imaginan?

ACC: *When were you rescued by the police? Where were you heading, Mr. García?*

R: Adonde mis **cachivachis** que tenía en un *RV* comprado en un **desguasadero** en *Yuma.* Yo no quería seguir cantando con los Los Hijos de Negrete ni con Los Zorrastros del Norte. Quería ser solista, ser libre. Los músicos son unos mezquinos, licenciada. No pagaban. Como le dije al licenciado de la defensoría, *Yuma Defendors, the RV* estaba parqueado en el *Blue Sky Ranch RV Park*, y **un cuate** me había dado residencia permanente en el estacionamiento sin pagar un centavo. Allí pernoctaba.

ACC: *And you were taken to a hospital, were you not, sir?*

R: Amanecí en el *Yuma county Detention Center* con algunas raspaduras, rasguños y heridas. ¡Ah! Tenía suturas en la nuca y moretones en la espalda. ¡Ah! Y una que otra costilla quebrada y en el tobillo derecho, también tenía unos rasponazos.

ACC: *So, where was it that ICE found you, Mr. García? And who exactly brought you to the detention center?*

R: En la carretera local, en la 95, en mismito *Yuma*. Iba yo en camino al cerro *Kofa*... Vivía en un *motor home* como le platiqué, señorita. **Pos** en la cárcel, allí pasé mis setenta y dos horas en la **hielera**. **Luego luego** me llevaron a una mazmorra y allí pasé una semanita. De la mazmorra me llevaron al centro de detención y allí me juntaron con **cuates** de Honduras, Guatemala, y hombres de la China.

IJ: *PROCEED, MS. LÓPEZ!*

ACC: *How is your mental health nowadays, Mr. García?*

R: No duermo. Me levanto con sofocones después de pesadillas de asfixia. Nunca antes tomé tanto tequila para dormir. Salvo pocas excepciones, **ahorita** necesito envenenarme cada minuto, digo desde que llegué a *Yuma*... aquí comencé a consumir lo que apareció, pastillas, alcohol, **mota**... Escucho voces también. Los **guachos** me siguen, mucha gente me persigue, guardias, veo gente armada que me sigue por callejones. Hay como demonios que me persiguen.

ACC: *Do you see a psychiatrist, Mr. García?*

R: ¡No! ¿qué es eso licenciada?

ACC: *Are you under medical care or under the supervision of any specialist, Mr. García?*

R: Sí, licenciada… hay dos señoritas que conversan conmigo…
ellas me visitan a menudo, una me da medicamentos y la otra
platica mucho conmigo.

ACC: *What medications are you taking?*

R: Una pastillita anaranjada, pero **ahorita** no recuerdo el
nombre.

IJ: *What are these medications for? Why are you taking them?*

R: *I don't know.*

BLOCK 8. Cross. Sonora cartels. Narcos. Drug trafficking.

ACC: *Sir, in your I-589 application you stated that, and I quote: "I did
not need to use any 'coyote' to cross into USA territory." Is that accurate?*

R: **¡Nel!** *True!*

ACC: *So, who is El Pollero Sásabe, Mr. García?*

R: **¡Va!** Un charlatán, pero de conocerlo no, no conozco a ese
pinche cabrón.

ACC: *Now, if you know, sir, when you lived in Altar, Sonora, or in any
other town in that state, was there present any recognizable drug cartel that
controlled the area?*

R: ¿Quién sabe? Los Federales son el cártel más grande en
Sonora. La DEA los dejó a cargo de Sonora. Mire, señorita,

donde hay plata hay corrupción. Los Federales y la DEA tumban un cártel y al ratico aparece otro, chiquito pero picoso.

ACC: *Mr. García, if you know, what kind of drugs do those small-time groups or* cabecillas *traffic in?*

R: De todo, señorita. Escuche usted, se mueve **ácido**, algunos le llaman **ajo**, se mueve puro *LSD*, el fentanilo, pastillas de todo tipo: oxicodona, Tramadol y muchas más, señorita.

(R pauses and looks at the window.)

ACC: ¡CONTINÚE SEÑOR!

R: Se mueve cocaína también que en la calle es la **fifi,** el **talco,** la **cremita**, eso es la cocaína en las calles.

(R pauses and looks at his right arm.)

ACC: *Mr. García, you had quite a résumé, a good résumé, one must say. You accrued a lot of experience working with narcos, building narco-mansions, mausoleums, tombs, tunnels. Is that fair to say, Mr. García?*

R: Trabajé en todas esas obras, señorita.

ACC: *So basically, you knew what everybody was doing in the trafficking business—who were the purveyors, providers, carriers of everything—and all that experience helped you. It was instrumental in you becoming a liaison for those businessmen or groups, right?*

R: *Right!*

ACC: *That is why you were the liaison between all the components of the drug distribution chain and you even advised some of the big honchos how to be efficient and successful. Right?*

R: ¡Añil! patrona.

ACC: *So, you were a narco who trained narco wannabes and helped big narcos, right, Mr. García?*

R: Yo no soy un narco, señorita. **Ahorita**, de la manera que usted lo pone, suena a película.

ACC: *So again, who did you work for while you were living in Mexico?*

R: Para mí, y para todo el que me pidió un favor y pagó su buena **lana**.

BLOCK 9. Cross. Lookout in the mountains. Security in the mines. Alias corroboration.

ACC: *Sir, when did you start working in the mountains as a lookout?*

R: Trabajé en los cerros sí. Fue, fue unos meses antes de empezar en los hoyos, y después de trabajar en **Querobai**.

ACC: *You were a lookout and later trained youngsters in that trade, right, sir?*

R: *Yes Ms. López!* ¡Sí, sí, sí! ¡Está en lo justo!

ACC: *You mentioned you worked in the mining industry. Were you full-time or part-time?*

R: Nunca **ponché** tarjeta, señorita López.

ACC: *How did you get paid? How did you receive your wages, sir?*

R: Me dieron *cash*, dinero sucio.

ACC: *Sir, how come you didn't write that in your affidavit in support of your own I-589?*

R: ¿No? Pues olvidó la Yooko. Yo conté mis historias y la señorita las **garabateó**.

ACC: *Sir, sir, remind me again: Who is Yooko?*

R: La señorita Quintanilla, señora. Yooko Quintanilla sirvió de intérprete, le conté las historias en **yaqui**, en español, hasta en inglés le conté historias. Seguro que la señorita olvidó escribir todas mis anécdotas y cuentos. Son muchas, muchas historias que tengo, agente.

ACC: *So, you are blaming Ms. Quintanilla for the omission of that story? Hard to believe, sir, but isn't it true that your I-589 application was read back to you in Spanish or another language that you understood and then you signed it, Mr. García López?*

R: Señorita, son muchos los papeles, muchas citas, muchas fechas, no sé qué pasó con ese artículo.

ACC: *How and where did you get the alias El Halcón?*

R: En el cerro, en la quebrada, en el desierto, en las obras, no sé, no recuerdo **ahorita**, señorita.

ACC: *Why and who called you El Halcón? How did that name come about?*

R: Porque siempre burlé la migra. Era rápido. Siempre escapé la migra, a los fronterizos. Nunca me atraparon.

ACC: *Mr. García, did you use other aliases besides the ones mentioned today in court?*

R: En las obras me llamaban El Güero. En la sierra, era El Güero García, y de vez en vez, el Halcón. Y bueno, Caraebarbie me llamaba el señorito Gaviota con quien tenía mucho roce. Él me llamaba Carabarbie o Caraniña, Carita, Cariño, Carababy, Caralinda, *Pretty Face*, CaraePan, *Sweet Face*, CaraeBebe, *Baby's Face*. Gaviota era un **yori**, señorita. El hombrín era un gringo extraño, señorita. Siempre de **buzo** o empastillado y se la pasaba coqueteando conmigo.

ACC: *Why would they call you Carabarbie or Baby Face, etc., etc., Mr. García López?*

R: Es la misma persona. No hay otro, señorita. Decía Gaviota que me parecía a una hembra, a mi hermana La Lupe, pero en realidad me parezco a la gemela, a Santa Ana. Siempre me

dijeron que me parecía a ella. Soy buen mozo, así dicen por ahí.

Mi cara no envejecía, no tenía arrugas.

ACC: *Have you ever been in jail in Mexico?*

R: **¡Añil!** señorita, un día. Pasé solo un día, en una celda

compartida.

ACC: *And how was the experience in the holding cell?*

R: Bien, pero no podía caer en la cárcel, no podía permitir que

me pusieran preso.

ACC: *Why?*

R: Intentarían violarme, señorita. No puedo arriesgarme a que

eso ocurra, señorita.

ACC: *But we all run that risk if we go to jail, Mr. García, isn't that*

right?

R: No con mi jeta de joven buen mozo, señorita, no.

(ACC smirks.)

ACC: *Mr. García, what makes your face so special?*

R: Fíjese usted que mi gemela Santa Ana y yo éramos idénticos.

¡Ya no! **Ahorita** soy hombre hecho y derecho y con mil arrugas.

De La Santa no sé nada. Anda perdida, no sé si le platiqué,

¿cierto?

(R pauses while ACC stares at him with a compassionate look.)

ACC: *You're the king of speculation, sir!*

BLOCK 10. Cross. Nicknames. Revisiting jobs performed by García López for the cartels.

ACC: *Mr. García, between the time you met with agent PZ and the time you left for Mexico City, what exactly did you do for the cartels?*

R: No trabajé para los cárteles, hice mis cambalaches y mis trueques, hice negocios con dueños de empresas, fábricas y grandes negocios, señorita. Conocía mucha gente y a cada quién le hice un favor. Hice mucho negocio. Así me gané la vida. Así pude informar a la Judicial, como ya le platiqué.

ACC: *So, at any point did you assist, aid or have any interaction with drug cartels or any transnational drug trafficking organization?*

R: Más tarde, cuando la Municipal de Altar me acusó de tener conexión con grupos del narco, entonces me convertí en la conexión entre la policía y los negociantes. PZ me facilitó el acceso a los jefes, a los peces gordos de cada negocio. PZ tenía contactos y me refirió a los grupos y hombres que la policía identificó como narcos. A partir de ahí yo serví como enlace con los traficantes y la prensa, y las parroquias, y los diputados, los políticos, y las alcaldías, y las fábricas, y talleres de chapistería y

mecánica, y aparcamientos de coches. Mi interacción creció.

Llegué a conocer mucha gente comprometida. ¿Me entiende?

Creo que ya les platiqué.

ACC: *What bosses are you referring by* peces gordos?

R: Un montón de ellos. Mire usted, le doy ejemplos: Tenemos a

un Gaviota, a un Chavito, de estos ya les platiqué, pero también

a **La Corcholata**, una borracha dueña de mozas de limpieza y

servicio de modelos, millonaria ella. Me relacioné con **La**

Coqueta, quien hacía banquetes, era la reina de la cocina en

Sonora. Me relacioné con **El Pollo**, dueño de fábricas de

conservas y embutidos. Me relacioné con **El Güero Toñito**,

ganadero y latifundista ¡Ah! promotor de carreras de **machos**.

Me relacioné con **El Patas**, fabricante de artículos de piel y

dueño de tiendas minoristas y comprador al por mayor de

artículos de vestir de cuero, dueño de almacenes también. Me

relacioné con **El Remix**, sonidista para fiestas, escenarios,

tarimas, y proveedor de luces para espectáculos. Era asociado de

Elvis, alias **El Bizco**, dueño de cantinas y distribuidor del mejor

bacanora sonorense. Tuve negocios con **CJ**, él exportaba

productos agrícolas, y bien conectado estaba con minoristas en

California. También hice negocios con **El Tuercas**, dueño de talleres de mecánica, conocido por importar autos nuevos y de uso. Era socio de **El Cochiloco**, propietario de imprentas, casas de giros y tiendas de empeño. Hice mis pesos con **El Pelos**, quien se dedicó al *Export-Import* productos químicos, fertilizantes, piroctecnia y fuegos artificiales para fiestas al aire libre. Enlisté en mis negocios a **El Bocinas**, editor de prensa local, y locutor de radio. Mucha plata hice con **El Tapón**, ganadero el señor y dueño de agencia de bienes raíces. Conocí y entablé amistad con **El Muñeco**, un chico muy valioso, multifacético, a veces hacía herrería, otras, trompeta de bandas, entrenador de artes marciales y hasta torero. Hice **business** con **El Orejas**, él era un quisquilloso fotógrafo, creador de páginas del internet, promotor y hacedor de retratos. Hice plata con **El Oso**, dueño de gimnasios y exportador e importador de equipos deportivos, dueño de agencia de viajes por ferris y vacaciones al exterior, y gestor de visados también. Muy bien me llevé con **La Alcancía**, mánager de un banco, certificado él en la economía y finanzas. Hice tratos con **El Pelón**, él tenía una agencia de guarda espaldas, y seguridad residencial. Le saqué plata a **El Huevo**, hacendado el hombre, dueño de granjas avícolas, ganado vacuno y bovino, importador de animales exóticos, aves y peces. Mis autos los arreglaba **El mofles**, chapista y mecánico. La plata corrió con **El Teletubbie**, dueño de una fábrica de enlatados. Me relacioné con **Pinocho**, ex alcalde de Altar, hoy día político de renombre en Sonora. Por supuesto hice billete con **El Caguamo**,[33] dueño de cerveceras locales, quien se desempeña en el negocio de importación de bebidas, este comenzó en el negocio de pipas y tanques de construcción, **dompes** de concreto premezclado, cemento a granel y al detalle y aún ofrece el servicio.

IJ: *Interpreter, could you tell us the meaning of those pseudonyms described by Mr. García or at least the best description you can offer?*

(R interrupts IJ.)

R: Son motes, señor magistrado. Sus nombres se los puedo escribir, pero necesito tiempo.

IJ: *INTERPRETER, PROCEED!*

ACC: *Mr. García, you mentioned you met El Chapo?*

---

[33] Apodos que solo un mexicano entendería. (19 de mayo, 2016). *La Gaceta Semanario de Sinaloa.* Recuperado de http://ww.semanariolagaceta.com/scgi-bin/noticias.cgi?Action=Viewdetails&Pk=10343

(R interrupts ACC.)

R: Conocí a Don Chapo señorita, **saurino** el viejo señor. **Don Chapo** es el chamán que con sus rezos me curó y me aconsejó ir al D.F. Y bien claro me dijo que no confiara de los **chilangos**, señores.

ACC: *Oh, I see! So, Mr. García, what kinds of drugs and quantities did you traffic?*

R: Cero, señores, cero… absolutamente nada, señorita. Se lo juro por la virgencita, créame usted.

(R makes the sign of the cross while talking.)

R: Es la verdad y nada más que la verdad. ¡Créame cuando se lo digo!

ACC: *Mr. García, your associates, the businessmen, the conglomerates, the cartels that afforded you the lavish lifestyle you enjoyed, the mansions, cars, pickup trucks, those individuals that you worked for—what type of cargo did they traffic in and out and what was the size of their shipments?*

R: Que quede claro que yo no moví carga alguna… yo nada más colaboré con los hombres del cártel, si no, ya hubiera **colgado el pico**, señorita. Ahora de que mueven, mueven de todo, señores… Los grandotes, los **meros, meros**, esos mueven carga al por mayor. En barcos, *trailers*, se mueven en aviones, señorita.

ACC: *How do you know that, Mr. García López?*

R: La prensa señor, lea la prensa y lo verá, se ve en la tele, en *Facebook*. La gente cotorrea también.

ACC: *Did you broker the purchase of any planes?*

R: Pos sí.

ACC: *Did you broker the purchase of any ships?*

R: Pos sí.

ACC: *Did you broker the purchase of any containers, trailers and other means of transportation?*

R: Claro que sí, donde hubo plata ahí estuve yo.

ACC: *Mr. García, while living in Mexico and at any time, were you charged for criminal conspiracy in relation to any collaboration you had with any drug cartels or criminal groups?*

R: ¿Mientras vivía en el D.F.?

ACC: *Throughout Mexico, anywhere in the entire country of Mexico.*

R: No, señorita.

ACC: *So, Mr. García, listen! Then how did you come to the attention of the judicial municipal police in Altar?*

R: Tenga en cuenta el factor venganza señor… Algunos de mis asociados, especialmente aquellos de grupúsculos que me debían plata, por no querer soltarla ¿qué se yo? Ellos fueron con chismes a la Municipal. Yo fui quien les había prácticamente enseñado a montar sus negocios, entonces se volvían glotones y no me pagaban. Pero terminaron mal, **pos**, eran los primeros que se iban al diablo... Lo tenían bien merecido. No me costaba nada soplarlos de mi camino, además aquel había sido el trato con las autoridades: informar. **Pos**, información tenían. Así mantuve ocupados a los oficiales que supuestamente me atendían, les mantenía distraídos, en definitiva, muchos de ellos cooperaban con cárteles, con los mismísimos grupos del hampa. Aquello era un juego de astucia y poder. Recibía entonces paga de las dos manos, señorita. Quién no me pagara los soplaba del camino.

BLOCK 11. Cross. A tunnel to San Diego. Guitars or weapons?

ACC: *Señor García, you said during direct examination that you entered San Diego on many occasions, right?*

R: Este, este, ¡así es! La primera vez entré de mañana por un túnel en Tijuana y ¡riata! a deshoras de la **nochi** ya estaba **del otro lado**. Por túnel sí, la primera vez y después muchas veces más, señorita. Seguro estoy que era San Diego. ¡**Añil**! Parecía aquello *Disney World*, no era ni **Hermosío** ni Guaymas no. **Pos**, la ciudad era muy diferente, se veía **padrísimo**, la gente, la vista, aquello no era el desierto, era una metrópolis.

ACC: *Mr. García, did you live in San Diego prior to entering the United States this last time around?*

R: ¡Nunca viví en ese estado no!

ACC: *Mr. García, are you sure?*

R: ¡Se lo juro por el diosito que está en el cielo! ¡No! Yo no me quedo donde no soy bienvenido.

ACC: *But Mr. García, yet you returned to the United States to live for good. Wasn't that the case?*

R: No me quedó otra, señorita. Me matan en Sonora si muestro mi jeta.

ACC: *Mr. García, couldn't you have then moved someplace else in Mexico and been safe?*

R: Pero no lo hice, señorita. Aquí estoy, no tuve otra.

ACC: *Did you make trips to San Diego other than by way of the tunnels?*

R: ¡Sí, claro! **Pos**, hice unos cuantos viajes por carretera, en *trailers*.

ACC: *During the trips you stated, before you made it to Arizona, did you purchase any significant number of weapons?*

R: No sabía qué se movía, pero armas iban y venían señor.

ACC: *Did you have permission from the U.S. government to come into the country?*

R: Tenía un pasaporte…

(ACC interrupts R and questions him.)

ACC: *Whose name was on that passport or passports, sir?*

R: NOMÁS MI NOMBRE.

ACC: *Sir, in the NTA your name appears as Jesús Antonio García López, not as Cuauhtémoc Infante Bernal?*

R: *Right!*

ACC: *So why Cuauhtémoc Infante Bernal—where did that name come from, sir?*

R: No recuerdo, señorita. Por aquel entonces era yo un **chavo**.

ACC: *Your passport shows thirty-three years of age, but you were probably twenty-four at the time.*

R: ¿Quién se acuerda?

ACC: *Your Honor, this is a two-part question. Jesús Antonio García López, were you the only driver during those trips made into Arizona, United States? And did you have purchase orders from any organization, company, store, individual or entity in Mexico?*

R: No, no, no, **El Patas** era el patrón, y yo el copiloto. Su nombre es Elvis pero lo llamaban **El Patas** porque pisaba duro el acelerador, y encima calzaba tejanas de gigante, aquel hombrín.

ACC: *Mr. García, you have a pretty good memory, but yet you don't remember the name in your own passport? Hard to believe, sir!*

R: Señorita, **El Patas** andaba con mi pasaporte durante la travesía.

ACC: *Did you ever use the name González in one of your passports, sir?*

R: José era el nombre que figuraba en uno de los pasaportes que me dio **El Patas**.

ACC: *Wasn't it Juan González, Mr. García, and why isn't that name listed in your I-589 as one of your aliases?*

R: Mi nombre es Jesús García, señora.

ACC: *Your name is Jesús Antonio García López, right?*

R: Cierto, García López.

ACC: *Sir, you have not answered my question. Why didn't you list the name Juan González on your asylum application?*

R: No tengo la menor idea. No creo que la intérprete me hizo esa pregunta cuando llenaba la aplicación.

ACC: *What kind of weapons did you carry in those trucks, Mr. García López?*

R: Yo vi cajas de guitarras, nada más.

ACC: *What do you mean by* guitars, *sir? Okay, how many boxes of guitars did you buy, sir?*

R: El último viaje fue en diciembre del dos mil doce o trece. El primer viaje lo hice con **El Caguamo**. Recuerdo que el **tata** me dejó manejar de regreso de *Yuma* cuando íbamos a cruzar por Andrade la frontera de México. El **Caguamo** se había empujado **mil chelas** a requeteprisa y **se puso pedo**; entonces me dijo, "agarra el timón y no pares hasta Nogales, güerito". Yo no tenía qué temer, pues el contenido eran guitarras, y cuánto podría valer la carga, pensé yo *¿right? In Yuma* habíamos ido a una tienda que se llamaba Guitarras y Cañones. Yo me quedé quieto en el camión y **El Caguamo** entró en la tienda. Imagino que allí compró las guitarras. Entonces se las aventaron al camión y nos largamos. **Luego luego** el hombrín me regaló un guitarrón. ¡Ah! Recuerdo que **El Caguamo** me hacía vendar los ojos y le tenía que dar conversación para mantenerle despierto. **El Caguamo** siempre **andaba pedo** de tanta **mota** que fumaba.

ACC: *So, either you or* **El Caguamo** *were under the influence while driving those trucks, sir?*

R: Entrando a Sonora, **El Caguamo** entraba ebrio y yo conducía el camión.

BLOCK 12. Cross. Who is the alleged twin sister? Who is Mr. García? Fast and Furious operation. Weaponry.

IJ: *After this brief recess, let's resume cross-examination and take it from your last question, Ms. López. Could you repeat your last question, please?*

ACC: *Mr. García, how come you didn't mention the existence of a twin sister? How is it that you didn't list your twin sister in your I-589?*

R: Como le platiqué, señorita, no sé de su vida de ella, no sé si vive o si está muerta… Yo sí le platiqué de mi hermanita a la secretaria Quintanilla cuando me interrogó. Ella tomó las notas en el bufete del señor abogado, *el Mr. Bollinger.*

ACC: *And, of course, Mr. García is the biological father of that twin sister and you, correct?*

R: No, el señor García me adoptó y nos dio sus apellidos.

ACC: *Can you shed some light as to why, Mr. García senior, your adoptive father, adopted you and your twin sister?*

R: Se dice que fuimos el resultado de amoríos de mi madre con un **yori**, mi madre tendría unos quince o dieciséis años. Al nacer yo, mi **tata**, el abuelo materno, no aprobó de nosotros y muy pronto nos separaron. Después de nuestro nacimiento, mi **tata** y la comunidad nos rechazó, no aprobaron de nuestra apariencia.

Una noche a mi hermana la enviaron a Nogales y días más tarde yo terminé en Cerro Carnero con tíos por parte de madre, familia bien lejana.

ACC: *What was in your appearance that made you look different, Mr. García?*

R: El color de la piel. Éramos **güeritos**, niños paliduchos donde la población era de piel canela, mucho más oscura. Parecíamos albinos, señor. Aquello fue mal visto, y siempre fuimos discriminados por eso, señorita.

ACC: *Sorry to hear about that tragedy, Mr. García. Did you ever get back to Altar?*

R: No regresé a Altar en mucho tiempo y tardé en reunificarme con mi gemela.

ACC: *Mr. García, were you in Sonora, Mexico, from 2012 until 2016?*

R: Sí, señorita.

ACC: *Mr. García, were you aware that the US conducted the Fast and Furious operation between 2012 and 2016 in the state you lived in during those years, in Sonora, Mexico? Were you collaborating with this mission in* *any capacity, more specifically with a covert operation of controlled traffic of weapons to Sonora from Arizona?[34]*

R: No conozco de ninguna misión rápida ni mucho menos furiosa. A partir de que me convertí en testigo clave para la municipal de Altar facilité transportación para mover armas, a grupos, llámele cárteles o sindicatos no sé. Aunque también compré armas de proveedores americanos, algunos de ellos hablaban español, chicanos ellos, otros hablaban un español raro.

ACC: *Do you remember the type of weapons and their characteristics, the weapons you dealt in while living in Altar, while being under protection by the municipal authorities?*

R: Los narcos piden El Cuerno de Chivo, el AK-47, es muy popular en el narco mundo, imagínese seis cientos disparos por segundo, es un arma muy vistosa, es un fusil de asalto ruso que nos llega de la frontera. Las ametralladoras *SAW 5.5* con capacidad de 700 disparos son demandadas. También el fusil R 15, ligerito y bueno para **levantones**, permite al narco soldado

---

[34] Redacción. (17 de Julio, 2011). El FBI pagó a narcos mexicanos como informantes. *Excelsior*. Recuperado de https://www.excelsior.com.mx/2011/07/17/nacional/753592#view-2

llevar más parque. Mire usted, también está la pistola belga, *la 5.7 de FN Herstal*, en la calle la conocen por "la matapolicías",[35] es desbastadora señorita. Los narcos pelean con bazucas, morteros de las mismísimas que usa el ejército norteamericano. Las granadas se compran de todos lados y causan grandes estragos, las granadas de fragmentación son letales; por un puñado de plata se consiguen. **¡Mal haya** la hora que las compré! El narco corre las calles con sus fusiles *Barret*, AR-15, granadas y lanzacohetes.[36]

ACC: *Where would you make most of the purchases, Mr. García?*

R: Yo no las compré. Yo las moví, las entregué más bien.

ACC: *Mr. García, the deliveries you just mentioned were made between what years?*

R: No sé, quizás en noviembre o diciembre del dos mil dieciséis, señorita.

---

[35] Paullier, J. (6 de mayo, 2015). ¿De dónde salen las armas pesadas del narco de México? *BBC NEWS/Mundo*. Recuperado de https://www.bbc.com/mundo/noticias/2015/05/150505_m exico_narcotrafico_carteles_origen_armas_jp

[36] Nájar, A. (25 de October, 2019). Narcotráfico en México: fusiles Barret, AR-15, granadas, lanzacohetes... los arsenales estadounidenses del crimen organizado mexicano. *BBC News/Mundo*. Recuperado de https://www.bbc.com/mundo/noticias-america-latina-50162346

ACC: *Were you aware that you were buying weapons from CIA undercover agents?*

R: No sabría decirle, solo sé que movía armas para muchos grupos, y todos eran hombres de negocios poderosos. ¿Narcos? No sé, indague usted con el agente PZ y los de la Municipal... y sí, había gringos envueltos en las movidas, señorita.

BLOCK 13. Cross. Informant for the FBI, CIA or DEA?
Segue to narcos, their pseudonyms: Who is who?

ACC: *Mr. García López, you testified earlier that you also used the alias Carabarbie. Right?*

R: ¡Solo esos maricas y sus hombres me llamaban Carabarbie, señorita!

ACC: *Who are you referring to by* faggots, *Mr. García?*

R: El güero Gaviota y Chavito eran **nahuilas**, afeminados ¿no se los platiqué?

ACC: *No, sir, no, you didn't refer to them as homosexuals in your oral testimony, nor in your written statements, Mr. García López.*

R: Más de una vez los vi en obscenidades en el picacho detrás del Elote. Son puros maricas, señorita.

ACC: *Okay, Mr. García, let's move to another set of questions. Did you ever work as an informant for the FBI, either before or after becoming an informant for the Mexican police?*

R: Este, este... yo trabajé para ciertos agentes, contados con los dedos de esta mano, señorita agente... Este, este, **pos** si ellos eran de la encubierta **del otro lado**, nunca lo supe, **pos** nadie me avisó.

ACC: *Did you work as an informant for the CIA?*

R: Como le platiqué anteriormente, cooperé con agentes en la Municipal, de la Estatal y con los Federales. Si eran *CIA*, no lo sé, señorita.

ACC: *Did you work as an informant for the Drug Enforcement Administration?*

R: ¿Cuál es esa señorita?

ACC: *DEA. I am referring to the United States federal law enforcement agency whose main objective is to go after traffickers of narcotics. Did you work for the DEA, Mr. García?*

R: No, a ellos no les vendí nada. Este, este… al menos, nadie nunca me informó.

ACC: *These questions are significant, Mr. García, and I want you to pay close attention to them. Did you work or not for the ex police officer, Miguel*

Ángel Félix Gallardo, aka El Jefe de Jefes and creator of some of the most powerful DTOs?

R: No, no, señorita.

IJ: *Interpreter, would you please translate the meaning of any aliases or pseudonyms given by any of the parties? Or, Mr. García, do you know if there's any meaning behind those pseudonyms?*

(ACC continues questioning R.)

ACC: *Did you work or not for the accountant and cartel leader Enedina Arellano Félix, alias La Jefa and the Tijuana Cartel?*[37]

R: Nunca escuché ese nombre, agente.

ACC: *Did you work or not for Antonio Cárdenas Guillén, alias Tony Tormenta from the Gulf Cartel?*

R: ¡Nel!

ACC: *Did you work or not for Jorge Eduardo Costilla Sánchez, alias El Coss from the Gulf Cartel?*

R: No, no, no.

ACC: *Did you work or not for Hector Beltrán Leyva, alias El Ingeniero, from the Beltrán Leyva Organization?*

---

[37] Grillo, Ioan. "Meet the First Woman to Lead a Mexican Drugs Cartel." Time. July 7, 2015. https://time.com/3947938/enedina-arellano-felix-tijuana. (Retrieve on November 27, 2020)

R: Este, este, no, nunca.

ACC: *Did you work or not for Edgar Valdez Villareal, alias La Barbie, a top lieutenant from the Independent Cartel of Acapulco?*

R: No creo.

ACC: *Did you work or not for Nazario "El Más Loco" Moreno González, from the New Family Michoacan?*

R: No me parece. Me parece que no.

ACC: *Did you work or not for José de Jesús Méndez Vargas, alias El Chango from the New Family Michoacan?*

R: No lo he oído mentar, señorita.

ACC: *Did you work or not for Servando "La Tuta" Gómez, from the Knights Templar Cartel?*

R: No lo he oído mentar tampoco, señorita.

ACC: *Did you work or not for Victor Hugo "El Tornado" Delgado Rentería from the Jalisco New Generation Cartel?*

R: *Never!*

ACC: *Did you work or not for Heriberto Lazcano, alias El Lazca from Los Zetas?*

R: Nunca, señorita.

ACC: *Did you work or not for Miguel Ángel Treviño Morales, alias Z-40 from Los Zetas?*

R: ¿Un **guacho**?

ACC: *No Sir, ex leader of Los Zetas.*

R: No lo conozco.

ACC: *Did you work or not for any member of the Gulf Cartel and their criminal outlet Los Zetas?*

R: No.

ACC: *Did you work or not for Joan Archivaldo Guzmán Loera, alias "El Chapo" and the Sinaloa DTO?*

R: Nunca.

ACC: *Have you worked or not for Los Chapitos, Mr. Guzmán's sons, Mr. García?*

R: No los conocí, no.

ACC: *Did you work or not for the lawyer and cartel leader Dámaso López Núñez, alias "Licenciado" and the Sinaloa Cartel?*[38]

R: No, agente.

---

[38] "Mexico: Organized Crime and Drug Trafficking Organizations." Congressional Research Service. Updated July 28, 2020. https://fas.org/sgp/crs/row/R41576.pdf (Retrieved on November 27, 2020).

BLOCK 14. Cross. Narco-mansions. Exhibit 34: a picture.

ACC: *Mr. García, in your visits to Mexico City, Zapopan, Jalisco or Culiacán in Sinaloa, did you ever visit any of the mansions or narco-mansions that have now been seized by the Mexican government?*

R: No creo, señorita. ¿Para qué señor?

ACC: *Whose picture is this, Mr. García? Your Honor, I am referring to Exhibit 34, Tab XX, on page 121, picture admitted into evidence as part of the evidentiary package for this asylum hearing, a picture of what looks like a man and his violin and a group of men with trumpets. Isn't that picture of you, Mr. García?*

R: No recuerdo haberme hecho esa foto, señorita agente.

ACC: *Now, Mr. García, isn't this your picture, the man with a violin in front of the Mexican-nationalized Chinese Zhenli Ye Gon's narco-mansion in Mexico City?*[39]

R: Se parece a mí, pero no toco ni trompeta ni violín, toco guitarra.

---

[39] Cave, Damien. "Inside the Homes of Mexico's Rich and Infamous." New York Times. January 18, 2012. https://www.nytimes.com/2012/01/19/garden/inside-the-homes-of-mexicos-alleged-drug-lords.html (Retrieved on November 12, 2019)

BLOCK 15. Cross. Cartel collusion.

ACC: *Mr. García, did you provide any aid or have any contact with the Sinaloa Cartel?*

R: ¡Nel! ¡Jamás!

ACC: *Mr. García, have you ever induced, assisted, abetted or colluded in the illicit trafficking of any controlled substance or trafficking of humans or weapons with the Gulf Cartel?*

R: ¡AH NO!

ACC: *Mr. García, have you ever induced, assisted, abetted or colluded in the illicit trafficking of any controlled substance or trafficking of humans or weapons with Los Zetas?*

R: ¡VA! ¡Ni modo! Y le estoy siendo honesto, señorita.

ACC: *Mr. García, have you ever induced, assisted, abetted or colluded in the illicit trafficking of any controlled substance or trafficking of humans or weapons with Los Caballeros Templarios?*

R: Nunca, licenciada.

ACC: *Mr. García, have you ever induced, assisted, abetted or colluded in the illicit trafficking of any controlled substance or trafficking of humans or weapons with the Jalisco New Generation?*

R: ¡Tampoco!

ACC: *Mr. García, have you ever induced, assisted, abetted or colluded in the illicit trafficking of any controlled substance or trafficking of humans or weapons with the Juárez Cartel?*

R: ¡Vaya una pregunta! ¡No señor!

ACC: *Mr. García, have you ever induced, assisted, abetted or colluded in the illicit trafficking of any controlled substance or trafficking of humans or weapons with the Beltrán Leyva Organization?*

R: ¡Ni madres señor!

ACC: *Mr. García, have you ever induced, assisted, abetted or colluded in the illicit trafficking of any controlled substance or trafficking of humans or weapons with La Familia Michoacana?*

R: A decir verdad ¡Negativo señor!

ACC: *Mr. García, have you ever induced, assisted, abetted or colluded in the illicit trafficking of any controlled substance or trafficking of humans or weapons with the Gulf Cartel?*

R: *Never!*

ACC: *Mr. García, have you ever induced, assisted, abetted or colluded in the illicit trafficking of any controlled substance or trafficking of humans or weapons with the Tijuana Cartel?*

R: No, señorita. ¡Jamás!

BLOCK 16. Cross. Trafficking methods.

ACC: *Mr. García, if you know, in how many ways did your associates traffic drugs or humans?*

R: De muchas maneras, señoritas. Por ejemplo, en latas de conservas se hace el tráfico. Yo facilité la transportación de láminas de acero para pequeñas fábricas de enlatados, vea usted. **Ahorita**, se comenta por ahí, que el pionero fue un señor, ya maduro, algunos le llamaban **El Soldador**, otros le conocían por **El Chapista**, nunca supe su nombre, pero le vi en compañía del Güero Buchón. Resulta que el hombre era dueño de un taller de chapistería, pero quebró y se dedicó a trabajar en talleres privados hasta que abrió su propia fábrica artesanal. **Pos, El Soldador** abrió su fábrica de enlatados en **Hermosío** y usando etiquetas **Comadre Jalapeños**, las rellenaba con cocaína, las sellaba al vacío y las expedía a mercados en California. Muchos mercaderes eran sus conocidos de Sonora, según dicen.[40]

ACC: *Were there any other methods that you're aware of?*

---

[40] Radden Keefe, Patrick. "Cocaine Incorporated." New York Times Magazine. June 15, 2012. http://www.nytimes.com/2012/06/17/magazine/how-a-mexican-drug-cartel-makes-its-billions.html (Retrieved on May 15, 2020)

R: Este, este, les voy a ser honesto, yo también gestioné flotas de camiones refrigerados, pienso que en ellas se traficó la carga. También se dice que, dentro de alimentos, como la sandía o el pescado de Baja California se metía la carga, pero también se envía por correo postal, por *FedEx*; por los cielos se mueve plata. Hasta aeromozas, las mismas azafatas que les llaman, ellas llevaban fajos de billete de un país a otro, señorita.[41]

ACC: *That's it, Mr. García? Do the cartels ship cargo in any other way to the United States?*

R: Hasta usan catapultas para lanzarlas al otro lado del murito, señor. El narco siempre se las arregla para enviar su paquetón, señorita.

ACC: *Mr. García, the smuggling takes place through the border, through the desert, isn't that true, Mr. García?*

R: En parte, pero la mayoría entra legal, entra por las garitas de San Ysidro en Tijuana, por Altar Sonora a *Sasabe Arizona*, de Nogales Sonora a *Mariposa Arizona* es otra. Hay muchos *gates,*

---

[41] Reyes, J.P. (15 de marzo, 2016). Cortan las alas a azafatas del Chapo; cae red de lavado en Colombia. *Excelsior*. Recuperado de https://www.excelsior.com.mx/NACIONAL/2016/03/15/108 0949

señorita. Hay más de cuarenta y tantas garitas a lo largo del borde, señorita.

ACC: *Do you know of any other methods to transport, traffic or smuggle drugs or launder money, Mr. García?*

R: ¿Blanqueo de capital? ¡Oh sí, sí, ya recuerdo! Mire usted, las azafatas de aviones comerciales son las que blanqueaban fajos de dinero, ya se lo platiqué a la Yooko. Pero, pero el tráfico también se hace por ferrocarril, se van en flotas de autos nuevecitos, de los acabados de ensamblar. Recuerdo recibir múltiples encargos de la *Ford*. Yo los iba a recoger a un parqueo en las afueras de **Hermosío**. Los compradores me pedían blancos con techo plateado. Entonces, los llevaba del parqueo al desguace, allí les escondían, allí estaban supuestos a embellecerlos y ponerles los juguetes que clientes de California pedían ponerle. La verdad era que allí le escondían la marihuana, y **luego luego** salían en ferrocarril a parqueos cerca de *Yuma, Arizona*. Usualmente en las ruedas va la marihuana o el narcótico. Pero se sabe que encargos como ese, se hacen a varios depósitos y concesionarios en **al**

otro lado. ¿No ha escuchado usted decir que los *Ford Fusion are dope?*[42]

BLOCK 17. Cross. Credibility. Mr. García López, a narco?

ACC: *So, Mr. García, would it be fair to say that you were known in the community as someone connected to the narcos and narcotrafficking?*

R: Sí, bueno, este, este… no, no, no, en realidad, no sé qué pensó la gente de mí pero yo sí vestía bien, a veces con camisetas o playeras polo, mis botas vaqueras de cuero de sapo o armadillo, con puntas bien largas, algunas de ellas les mandé a hacer sus logotipos dorados que decían, Güero o GG o Güero García, muy vistosas por cierto. Mis correas tenían hebillas grandotas y relucientes. También me ponía mis camisas de ceda de la *Barabas Fantasy*, muy **fachosas**, esas con patrones de colores estaban muy de moda y las tenía para lucir en fiestas y **rochelas**. Del cuello me colgaba mi cadenón de oro, con la virgencita en el pecho, y en mi muñeca llevaba una gorda pulsera de oro, señorita. Y el diente de oro que aún luzco, eso es

---

[42] Andone, Dakin. "$1 Million in marijuana found in brand new Ford Fusions." July 16, 2017. CNN. https://www.cnn.com/2017/07/16/us/marijuana-ford-fusion/index.html (Retrieved on May 15, 2020)

tradición señor. Pero mis **trocas** tenían el logo, *Constructora Querobabi*, así que nadie pudo identificarme como narco si no como constructor, pero con mucha **lana**.

ACC: *Mr. García, you even stated in your affidavit of support that the municipal police thought you were connected to the cartels. Can you explain?*

R: ¡No sé por qué! Mira que hay soplones por todos lados, señorita. También, hay muchos impostores, señorita. También, hay mucha competencia; es un todo contra todos, se lucha por ganar plata y no falta la gente envidiosa. Así que cualquiera pudo haber informado a la local de mis negocios.

ACC: *But you ended up working, cooperating and joining forces with the police. As a matter of fact, in your testimony today and your written testimony as well, you state that you became a key witness in the investigations in the municipality of Altar in Sonora, right?*

R: Dije eso sí, y está escrito de mi puño y letra.

ACC: *Mr. García, you in fact became a cooperating witness at the federal level, and for that matter they provided you with protection in a building called Zócalo, right?*

R: Este, cierto es licenciada.

ACC: *Mr. García, no one thought you were and you never acted as a policeman, and you never dressed or carried police weaponry as one, right, Mr. García?*

(R pauses.)

D: *OBJECTION!*

IJ: *Sustained!*

ACC: *I'll move on, Your Honor. Mr. García, once you surrendered to ICE and once you were interviewed, didn't you express your willingness to provide information about the Carabela Cartel?*

R: No entiendo, señorita.

ACC: *I'll rephrase the question. You were interviewed by ICE several times, and during those interviews you provided lots of information about activities carried out by important capos of the drug trade, whether you knew they were capos or not. Now, didn't the capos from the Carabela Cartel provide you with material information to mislead and misguide the efforts of the DEA, Sir?*

R: Esto, este, ¡pos no! Déjeme serle honesto, bien honesto, señorita. No, yo no recuerdo platicar con alguien de ese cártel, señorita.

ACC: *So you lied to ICE agents as well, Mr. García. Wasn't that the same approach you had back in the municipality of Altar that you even* *stated in your written testimony and oral testimony just minutes ago,*

Mr. García? And I quote: "During the first meetings at the judicial I

informed or misinformed, particularly agent PM from the police

department," Sir?

R: ¿PM?

ACC: *YES!*

R: No, señorita. Yo solo hablé con el agente PZ.

ACC: *Did the Carabela Cartel offer you information to provide to the*

American authorities?

R: ¡Le digo que no! Esa es la mera verdad.

ACC: *You also stated, in your oral and written statement: "I thought that*

by doing that the police would have an excuse to investigate and raid those

groups that played a minor role around my radius of action."

R: Este, creo que es verdad que así pensaba, señorita fiscal.

ACC: *Did Bachia Banderas provide any affidavit in support of your*

asylum application, Mr. García?

R: ¿Bachia? ¿Quién sabe de esa **morra**?

ACC: *Did Mary Lourdes Carney provide any affidavit in support of your*

asylum application, Mr. García?

R: ¿Para qué?

ACC: *Did Pancha García provide an affidavit in support of your asylum application, Mr. García?*

R: ¿Pancha Morales?

ACC: *Pancha Morales, your older sister, Mr. García, the one who lives in Alaska. Aren't you in touch with her, sir?*

R: Puedo pedírselo, señorita.

ACC: *Did either Alma or Bernarda provide an affidavit for your asylum application, Mr. García?*

R: ¿Mis medias hermanas?

ACC: *YES, MR. GARCÍA LÓPEZ!*

R: Ellas son agraciadas señoritas, ellas se fueron a Culiacán y allá se desposaron con meros meros del 89.

ACC: *Del 89, Mr. García—what do you mean by that?*

R: Pos, del mismísimo Sinaloa Cártel 89 señorita.

BLOCK 18. Cross. Last chapter: Zócalo.

ACC: *Mr. García, I am going back to when you spent time in Zócalo, under the safeguards of the Mexican federal authorities.*

(R interrupts ACC.)

R: ¿Dónde?

ACC: *Sir, let me finish asking the question. I am referring to the shelter for whistleblowers, okay? Now, were you aware that Mr. Pena, el teniente—the guy that you testified earlier seemed to be from Monterrey because of his accent and use of colloquialisms—were you aware that he was a DEA agent?*

R: No nunca supe que era un encubierto. Él actuaba como un mero **pochi** de Monterrey; pero medio **cuatrero**, un poco extraño, medio tartamudeaba y algunas palabras no se les entendía. Sí, tartamudo el hombrín.

ACC: *Mr. García, has anyone on your behalf, that is to say, any law enforcement agency in the United States, filed any petition for you to become a permanent resident?*

R: Ni modo, licenciada.

ACC: *What are you afraid of, Mr. García López?*

R: No puedo regresar a Sonora.

ACC: *Can you return to Mexico and live safely in any state other than Sonora?*

R: No creo señorita, esos canallas se meten en cada hoyo. Se lo he dicho una y mil veces, señorita.

(R starts crying.)

ACC: *Who are you afraid of, Mr. García?*

R: A los narco-federales, a la muerte, al calabozo.

End of cross-examination by Ms. López.

IJ: *Now I'd like to hear closing arguments from the respondent's attorney,*

Mr. Bollinger, and the attorney from Department of Homeland Security,

Ms. López.

End of "The Hearing."

Happy Interpreting!

I hope you have found this manual instructive and useful.

If you have any questions or comments, feel free to email at: manualvolume1@protonmail.com.

GLOSSARY

a) Palabras de origen Yaqui

Bachia: Antes. // Prioridad, preferencia. // Semilla.

Bejo'orim: Lagartija.

Chapayeka: Fariseo.

Huotepoli: Mosquito.

Jiawai: Música, ritmo, sonido, tono. // Armonía. // Eco.

Kari: Casa, finca.

Kawis: Zorro.

Kokowame: Muerte.

Maaso: Venado cola blanca.

Naawa: Raíz. // Causa, principio. // Base, origen.

Nacabochi: Del cahita. *naca,* oreja. Del ópata *pochi,* corto, recortado.

Tajkaim: Tortilla.

Tekia: Oficio.

Tomi: Dinero.

Wakabaki: Caldo tradicional yaqui.

Yori: Hombre blanco.

b) Vocabulario sonorense

Acequia: Canal de riego de pequeña escala.

Échame agua: Vigila e informa.

Al otro lado: A los EEUU.

A poco: Expresión admirativa que rechaza implícitamente un despropósito.

Amalaya: (¡Ah mal haya!). Se expresa deseo vehemente por medio de una maldición.

Andaba pedo: Borracho.

Antiparras: Gafas.

Añil: Afirmación.

A ráis: Sin protección.

A trochis mochis: (A mata caballo) Indica que algo se ha hecho en forma improvisada y a la ligera.

Ay nomás: Ciertamente.

Babosada: Necedad, tontería.

Bacanora: Aguardiente que se obtiene del maguey sonorense.

Baile de monte: Designa al tipo de baile en que alguien lo financia personalmente y luego éste le cobra una cuota a cada pareja.

Bato: Jovenzuelo.

Bártulos de aturdida: Soñadora.

Bobito: Houtepoli. Mosquito.

Boñigas: Estiércol.

Borreguero: Dícese del que suelta especies falsas, embustes, o patrañas.

Bramona: Sonido onomatopeyico emitido por el ganado vacuno.

Buzo: Ebrio.

Caballos de Cuarto de Milla: Raza de caballo.

Cacalbro: Embaucador, timador, engañador, arbitrista.

Cachivache: Trastos.

Cachucha: Gorra.

Caíta: interj. 1. Palabra para indicar que algo con que se contaba, en realidad no existía en ese momento. 2. Para manifestar frustración.

Cantón: Hogar, casa.

Capsules: Los capsules. Casquillos de balas.

Carajal: Multitud, grupo numeroso.

Carajada: Acto propio del granuja, del tunante, forma derivada del vulgarismo carajo.

Castigada: La castigada. El castigo.

Cate la boca: Contracción de la frase "Cáyate la boca".

¡Cate monte ilichi!: ¡Estate quieto!

Chamuchina: Grupo numeroso de muchachos.

Chante: Casa.

Chanza: Oportunidad.

Chapo: Chaparro.

Charanga: Automóvil viejo y estropeado.

Chirinolera: Chismosa.

Chisgues: Vestimenta demasiado informal, "de fachas".

Checaron: Revisar.

Chirinolera: Chismosa.

Chisgues: Vestimenta demasiado informal, "de fachas".

Chismarajo: Chisme grande, enredo complicado.

Chonte: Diminutivo de zenzontle.

Chopa: Borracho, ebrio, teporocho.

Chorcha: La chorcha. Iglesia. Del inglés church.

Chota: Policía.

Choyaca: Matocha. Moretón o hinchazón donde se ha formado una llaga.

Chupar: Fumar.

Churi: Niño o adolescente. (También ver Churea en Diccionario de Saborza, Horacio)

Clavar el pico: (colgar el pico) Morir.

Cochi: Cerdo.

Codosduro: Cicatero.

Corridas: Acto de reunir el ganado que anda en campo abierto.

Corriendito: Diminutivo del gerundio corriendo.

Cotorro: Dícese de la persona de soltería avanzada.

Covacha: Pequeña cueva formada generalmente debajo de algún peñazco.

Coyota: Pastel de masa de trigo. Es una especie de empanada de color moreno y de gusto agradable. El modismo alude a la mujer llamada coyota, hija de india y español.

Criaturero: Conjunto de buquis.

Cuatrero: Ladrón.

Cuesco: Cogote.

Cuico: Policía.

Cúmaro: Árbol corpulento que abunda en Sonora, de tronco derecho y madera dura.

De nacencia: De nacimiento.

De parte tarde: Horas después del mediodía.

Dogos: Hot dogs.

Dompe: (Domper) Volquete moderno provisto para arrojar tierra y materiales de construcción.

Edá: Expresión que se utiliza para confirmar la veracidad de un hecho.

Ehui: Sí

Enchalecar: Apropiarse, adueñarse de algo ajeno.

Estacionómetro: Aparato que mide el tiempo de estacionamiento de un auto.

Fachoso: Dícese del que muestra afectación en el vestir, en sus ademanes o gestos; del que carece de sencillez en su porte; del que presume de elegante, de buen parecer.

Fajina: Faena.

Flance: Prometida.

Fondeado: Adinerado.

Gallina Pinta: Sopa sonorense.

Garabatear: Hacer garabatos o escribir apresuradamente y con mala letra.

Generoso: Tipo de caballo con paso de ambladura o andadura, lo cual lo hace muy apreciado.

Guachos: Los guachos. Se le llama despectivamente al soldado federal.

Guarachar: Bailar.

Güilo o Huilo: Delgado.

Hermosío: Hermosillo.

Hielera: Celda frígida.

Horruras: Sobras.

Insultada: La insultada. El insulto.

Jaina: Novia.

Jiruto: Desnudo.

Jodazo: Golpe.

Leperuza: *La leperuza.* La clase malviviente.

Machos: Caballos.

Macuchi: Tabaco de calidad inferior cultivado en las márgenes del río Yaqui.

Mainates: Líderes.

Menjurges: Maquillajes.

Mentidero: Lugar de reunión.

Menudo: Sopa sonorense.

Mmmta: Interjección de enojo o coraje.

Morra: Muchacha.

Nahuila: (nagüila) Afeminado.

Nel: No, negación.

Nochi: Noche.

Nomás que: Luego que, inmediatamente, solamente.

Noraguas: Clientes, merchantes.

Oscurana: Dícese del color oscuro que adquieren las nubes y su alrededor ante una inminente tormenta.

Ópata: Grupo indígena que habita en las montañas de Sonora.

Pacota: Conjunto de chamacos.

Pascola: Baile de los indios de la raza cahita. // El danzante mismo y, cuando son varios, el principal. Esta forma deriva de "páscoa" y "pasco", fiesta. Tal locución no es sino alteración de "Pascua", forma aquella que coincide con la portuguesa "páscoa" (Ignacio Zúñiga).

Pachocha: Pochi.

Penco: Estúpido.

Pincel: A pie.

Pinchi: Individuo de poca calidad moral.

Pisto: Unos pistos. Tragos.

Pochi: Agringado.

Ponchar: Reportar el horario en tarjeta de entrada y/o salida laboral.

Rajuela: Cuchara de albañil.

Ranfla: Carro, camioneta, troca, pick up.

Recalar: Regresar al punto de partida.

Resolana: Calor sofocante provocado por el sol durante el verano en espacios abiertos.

Resortera: Tirador: Artefacto para lanzar objetos.

Retinto: Dicho de un animal: De color castaño muy oscuro.

Retobado: Mulo, terco, desobediente, malcriado.

Riata: Interjección que usa para enfatizar golpe recibido.

Rochelas: Reunión, tertulia, mentidero donde alegremente se picotea y chismorrea.

Ruñir: Roer.

Saurino: Adivino.

Seguranza: Seguro.

Señales de sangre: Marcar el ganado.

Soltar un borreguero: Rumor que se extiende en alguna región dando a conocer alguna noticia, generalmente de fondo morbosa y casi siempre resulta falsa.

Tanichi: Tienda de abarrotes.

Tata: Anciano.

Tatema: Cabeza.

Tecolines: Dinero. Moneda.

Testito: Lleno de buitres.

Tiriciento: Triste, abatido.

Tracamandanga: Tramposo, embaucador; mexicanismo: tracalero.

Triquitrate: Disparos de arma de fuego.

Trochil: Pocilga, porqueriza.

¡Va!: ¡Cómo no!

Viborona: Mañosa, artera.

¡Vóytelas!: Exclamación de sorpresa.

Vuqui o Buqui: Niño.

Vucada: Grupo de niños o muchachos.

Zaino: Caballo de color café claro.

Zorrastrón: Tipo de bajo sentido moral, granuja, zascandil, hábil en trapacerías.

c) Narcolengüaje

Ácido: Droga alucinógena elaborada principalmente a partir de un derivado sintético del ácido lisérgico.

Alijo: Reserva oculta.

Arponearse: Injectarse.

Buchón: Narco-junior; que vive de acuerdo a la cultura del crimen organizado.

Burrero: Contrabandista de drogas.

Churro: Cigarro de marihuana.

Darse un pericazo: Consumir cocaína.

Encobijado: Féretro cubierto en mantas o sábanas.

Feria: El cambio, vuelto.

Fifí, talco o cremita: cocaína.

Gomero: Extrator de la goma de la amapola para la confección de la cocaína.

Lana: Dinero.

Levantón: Secuestro de uno o más miembros de una pandilla rival u otro enemigo.

Lona: Narco-blanket.

Luego luego: Enseguida.

Llave: *Troca con llave.* Camión con cuernos instalados en la defensa.

Mota: Marihuana.

Narcomantas: Pancarta, cartel usado por los narcos para intimidar a sus víctimas.

Perico, Gallo y Chiva: Cocaína, marihuana y heroína.

Polleros: Traficantes de humanos (human *traffickers*).

Punteros o Halcones: Vigía, centinela, vigilante.

Requintar: Acusar.

Resollar: Respirar.

Sapo: Soplón.

Tabique: Ladrillos de marihuana compactada.

Topos: Abre túneles.

d) Vocabulario de origen nahua-azteca

Atole: Atol. Bebida caliente.

Chinamen: Jacal de petate.

Cuate: Camarada, amigo, íntimo.

Machihui: Revoltijo de comida sobrante de varios platos. Comida para cochis preparada a base de los remanentes de varios platillos.

Tzapa: Enano.

e) Jerga del país.

Ahorita: Ahora.

Chamba: Empleo, Trabajo.

Chava(o): Niña(o), pequeña(o).

Chela: Cerveza.

Chilango: Que es originario de la ciudad de México.

Chingada: *Los hijos de la chingada madre.* Los hijos de puta.

Corralón: Terreno donde la Policía guarda los vehículos retirados por estacionar en lugares prohibidos.

Deshuesadero: Lugar donde se acumulan los coches inservibles para ser desmantelados o desarmados.

Desmadre: Confusión.

Güero: Dicho de una persona: Que tiene los cabellos rubios.

Mamón: Que trata de hacerse el gracioso, de quedar bien sin tomar en cuenta la situación o que presume de sí mismo sin considerar la situación en que lo hace.

Mero: justo, preciso.

Mero mero: El más fuerte, poderoso, principal.

Padrísimo: Óptimo.

Pinche: Maldito.

Plebe: Niño.

Pos: Pues.

Bibliography

Glossary Sources

Buitimea Valenzuela, C., et al. (2016). *Diccionario yaqui de bolsillo. Jiak noki-español/ Español-Jiak noki.* Hermosillo, Sonora: Universidad de Sonora. (Colección lingüística: Serie 7. Estudios lexicográficos). Recuperado de https://www.researchgate.net/profile/Zarina_Estrada-Fernandez/publication/319873078_Diccionario_yaqui_d e_bolsillo_Jiak_noki-espanolEspanol-Jiak_noki/links/59be99d50f7e9b48a29881b5/Diccionari o-yaqui-de-bolsillo-Jiak-noki-espanol-Espanol-Jiak-noki.pdf

De la Torre, J. (23 de mayo, 2006). *Real Academia de la Lengua Sonorense.* Recuperado de http://www.jorgedelatorre.net/cultura/diccionario/Diccio narioSonorense2006_05_2312.pdf

Lara, L.F. Diccionario del español usual en México. *Biblioteca Virtual Miguel de Cervantes.* Recuperado de http://www.cervantesvirtual.com/nd/ark:/59851/bmc2 n5h9

Sobarzo, H. (Ed. Digital 2016). Vocabulario Sonorense. *Gobierno del Estado de Sonora, Instituto Sonorense de Cultura, Editorial Universidad UNILÍDER.* Recuperado de https://www.unilider.edu.mx/vocabulario-sonorense/

El lenguaje narco llega a los diccionarios mexicanos. (8 de agosto, 2016.). *El Observador.* Recuperado de https://www.elobservador.com.uy/nota/el-lenguaje-narco-llega-a-los-diccionarios-mexicanos-20168816300

"El Macho". *¡Conoce Sonora Compa!* (Blog). Recuperado de http://conocesonoracompa.blogspot.mx/p/generalidade s-de-sonora.html

Gabón, E. (31 de julio, 2014). Historia y resistencia de la tribu yaqui. (Blog). Recuperado de http://www.rebelion.org/noticia.php?id=187930

El Faraón. (2009). Diccionario de Regionalismos. El habla popular en la sierra de Sonora. (Blog). Recuperado de https://laradioladehernan.blogspot.com/2012/07/diccio nario-de-regionalismos.html

Robinson, M.F., Charlene Jones-Reid y Lopez. *Mexican Slang plus Graffiti* (Book). San Diego: Sunbelt Publications; 2003.

Ellingwood, Ken. "Grim glossary of the narco-world." Los Angeles Times. October 28, 2009. http://articles.latimes.com/2009/oct/28/world/fg-narco-glossary28 (Retrieved December 4, 2018)

Acknowledgements

This book is the product of the efforts of many people. In particular, we appreciate the rigorous legal edits of Teresa Statler Carone, Esq. and the line editing and proofreading done by Browne Editorial Department.

The publisher takes responsibility for any remaining errors.